BOOTS BELTS BERETS

Tanushree is a self-confessed word-a-holic and a traveller. When not reading or writing books, she's sure to be packing her bags and boots to zip around the world. A true maverick, she stumbled through many career choices before settling on writing.

A chocolate addict with a penchant for the unusual, she has collected dozens of interesting certificates that range from a wine-master's assistant at Australia, an international reindeer driving licence from Lapland, to one from 'The School of Hard Knocks' at Royal Selangor.

After leading a nomadic life for several decades, thanks to the Indian Army, she has finally grown roots at Pune. Tanushree can be contacted on her website – http://www.tanushreepodder.com

BOOTS BELTS BERETS

Tanushree Podder

ROLI

First published in 2008
Ninth impression, 2024

Roli Books Pvt. Ltd.
M-75, Greater Kailash II Market, New Delhi 110 048
Phone: +91 (011) 40682000
E-mail: info@rolibooks.com
Website: www.rolibooks.com
Also at Chennai & Mumbai

ISBN: 9788186939383

Typeset by Photina MT Roli Books Pvt. Ltd.
Printed in New Delhi, India

~

For all cadets of NDA – past, present and future – the sentinels and pride of our nation

~

ACKNOWLEDGEMENT

I am grateful to my husband for allowing me to intrude into the memories of his Academy days. Like a true officer and a gentleman, he stuck to his gallant offer of seeing me through the gruelling hours of work.

AUTHOR'S NOTE

This book comes with a caveat. If you are young, adventurous, impressionable and eligible, and receive an invitation to attend the POP (Passing Out Parade) at the National Defence Academy (NDA), Khadakvasala, Pune, don't accept it, because if you do, you are most likely to return to it as a cadet one day. The POP works its magic on young blood. It evokes patriotic emotions, makes you proud of being an Indian, and reminds you of your calling.

The POP can perhaps take the credit for bringing in more cadets, each year, than the high-flying advertisements in the media released by the Ministry of Defence.

Without doubt, the Indian defence services are the best in the world. And I would say, better even than the Sandhurst of the UK, and the West Point of the USA. Geopolitically, our country is at a disadvantage, as some neighbouring countries have displayed hostile tendencies in the last half-century.

It is to the credit of our armed forces that we have always managed to emerge the winners in most conflict situations. It is the NDA that deserves the credit for turning boys into real men.

Turning out lean, mean, and clean toughies with hearts of gold, is not a small feat. The ragging, punishments, and hardships are just a part of the game, taken by the cadets in their stride.

With the mysterious aura around the army, it is not surprising that most civilians are clueless about army life, and have fanciful notions about it. I do not blame them. Although I have been married to an army officer for a long time now, there are certain facets of army life that still baffle me. It is the same with most wives – believe me. I spoke to many of them about this and they agreed that there is so much we do not know. The time spent at the National Defence Academy, for instance. It seems to hold a special significance for the officers, whether they are in the army, navy, or the air force. The bonding between the course mates is eternal, and so are the memories.

The idea about this book occurred when we were posted in Bangalore. Since there were quite a few of my husband's NDA course mates posted in the city, they decided to meet regularly on Saturday nights. As I watched them going back in time, I realized how much it meant to them. They were as excited as the teenagers who went into the Academy on the first day. Notes were exchanged, secrets revealed, weaknesses disclosed, and nicknames divulged amidst much banter. In the beginning, I was jealous ... simply envious. I felt like an intruder who had barged into a fun party. The language, the codes, and the jokes they shared, made no sense to me. Watching the camaraderie between them, I realized that their years at the NDA would always remain the best phase of their lives.

Along with that realization came the awareness that there was so much I did not know about my husband's life at the Academy. It was a hidden facet of his persona that sounded too interesting to overlook. I decided to find out as much as I could about it. Although my husband had shared many experiences and memories of his days at the Academy with me, there were many gaps that needed to be filled in. To say that the NDA days were a high point in his life, would not be an exaggeration because all that came later, fell flat before the adventures and experiences shared at the Academy.

During a vacation, I began goading him to narrate the story of his Academy days. I began making notes at the end of each session, surreptitiously. The idea was to surprise him with a book about his experiences at the Academy. At the end of the vacation, I discovered a huge cache of anecdotes and other experiences. I knew that it had to be shared by everyone, and so, I went to work. Prodding him to reveal the details was just one of the hurdles; putting them together was a major challenge.

The book is set in the 1970s, during the time my husband was training at the Academy. It was the time when Pune was called Poona, and Mumbai, Bombay. It was a time when Rajesh Khanna was the teenagers' heart-throb and the Big B was nowhere in the reckoning; getting above seventy per cent marks was considered superlative, and there were no computers around. The concept of control, alt, delete had not hit mankind, nor had video games inhibited youthful minds. Jaya Bhaduri, foreign jeans, and discotheques, were the rage.

There were twelve squadrons in the NDA at that time. The boys came into the Academy straight after passing high school, and were very young. My husband joined at the age of fifteen and a half after tackling the entrance examination, which is as tough as the ones for engineering or medical schools. Ragging was backbreaking, and called for a lot of courage to face. Today, ragging has almost disappeared, except for a few stolen moments of good fun. In keeping with the times, there is a more liberal approach towards everything. Much seems to have changed in the Academy, and yet, nothing has actually changed. The ethos, training, and the attitude remain the same.

I am sure all the officers who have gone through the

Academy will identify with the episodes, and the 'wannabe' officers would find them inspirational. Life at the Academy retains the same moments of fun and pain, as starry-eyed, patriotic youngsters pass through it each year, their dreams intact, and their experiences priceless. Writing about the experiences at the Academy, was the best gift I could have given to my husband as well as his friends. Cheers to the NDA!

ONE

It was 9.00 a.m. The morning was crisp and the atmosphere businesslike that July, on the platform of the Poona railway station. It had rained all night, and the station building appeared as though it had been washed clean, its exterior cleared of the accumulated cobwebs, soot and dust. Puddles of water had collected in a few places where leaks had sprung up in the roof.

Tea vendors jostled newspaper hawkers, toy sellers elbowed fruit vendors, and all around was a melee of human limbs. Snack-laden trolleys occupied centre stage, thronged by hungry voices clamouring for breakfast. A cacophony of confused voices, punctuated by the rumble of passing trains, assaulted the eardrums. Trains passed through the platforms, spewing out weary passengers even as fresh hordes of people jumped into them, enthusiastic and cheerful. Hours later they would emerge, tired and dishevelled, at their destination. The fetid air, thick with the smell of urine, stale food, cigarettes, perspiration, and dirt, circulated in the freshness of the morning.

Like a giant caterpillar, another train weaved its way on to the track, abutting on platform number one, and disgorged, along with other passengers, a load of about a dozen boys from its entrails – all of them gangly teenagers, about sixteen to seventeen years of age. Their eyes shining with enthusiasm, the stance upright, their restless limbs bursting with energy, these travellers were different. They were not like the tired, perspiring, and dishevelled lot of humanity who flitted around the platform. The youthful energy of the boys flooded the platform, purging the murky atmosphere around it.

I was one of them.

I glanced at the motley collection of passengers spread around platform number one. Some of them were walking about, stretching their limbs; some brushing their teeth near the water taps, gargling and spitting loudly. A few were purchasing breakfast from the vendors, and eating them from the plates fashioned out of leaves. The tea stall did brisk business, as did the newspaper hawker.

Nervously, I fingered the neatly folded letter lying in my pocket. We would be met at the station, it stated. Looking around, I spotted a kiosk marked 'Reception Centre', on one side of the platform, and made my way towards it.

My heart was suffused with pride as I saw the letters 'NDA' stamped on the banner above the counter. Smart-looking men uniformed in the three colours of army, air force, and navy, bustled around the stall. They were stationed there to help the newcomers, and direct them to the Academy.

Cautiously, I looked around. A couple of other boys, weighed down by their signature black tin trunks, were moving uncertainly towards the counter. At the last count, there were about ten of us walking towards it.

Easy, chap, easy! I admonished my fast-beating heart, and strode decisively to the reception centre. My hands felt clammy with nervousness as I approached the reception committee.

What do I tell them? I wondered.

The opening line, stupid, think of a good and smart opening line! whispered my inner voice.

Hi, I have been selected to join the NDA, I mumbled to myself. Not a good line. *Should I begin with a greeting? Something like, Hi, I am Nikhil Dutta!*

The palms felt clammier. By now, my lungs were full of unexpelled air. I was hyperventilating.

I need not have bothered. The other boys had already lined up before the counter by now. No one paid attention as I joined the lot. A couple of girls passed by, throwing smiles our way, smiles that brightened my day. My nervousness dissipated a bit, and the cloud lifted from my mind. Too preoccupied to grin back at the girls, I smiled timidly at the boy standing next to me. The smirk he returned was equally uncertain, but a silent bond sprung up between the two of us, linking our predicament. More boys emerging from a multitude of trains joined us after a while.

As soon as about twenty-five of us had gathered at the reception centre, we were led to a bus earmarked for our destination. The baggage, as instructed in the letter, was identical – a black metal trunk with our names painted on it, and a bedding-holder. The other items such as airbags and water bottles, were optional. These were loaded on an army truck.

We headed for the National Defence Academy, Khadakvasala, about twenty kilometres away from the railway station. I can't say what the others felt, but I had a funny sensation in the pit of my stomach, as though I was seated on a giant roller-coaster hurtling downwards. This feeling lasted till I stepped on the hallowed ground of the Academy, and gaped at the surroundings. Going by the expressions on the faces around me, I can vouch that a similar sensation must have gripped the guts of the other boys. The Academy, with its beautiful structures, was clean, green and orderly – an impressive set-up. And soon, I was going to be a part of it.

All of a sudden, my chest swelled, and the constriction vanished. I was overwhelmed by a sensation more overpowering than nervousness – pride.

We had been offloaded in front of the mess. To civilians, it must be a mystery why such grand club-like places are known as 'messes' in the defence services. I have often wondered myself.

In the meanwhile, a second bus arrived from the Khirkee railway station, and another twenty-five lanky teenagers spilled out of it. They joined us as we stared, awestruck, at the derelict fighter aircraft, and the captured enemy battle tank, placed on the mess grounds.

Barely had we finished the tea and snacks served so thoughtfully to us by the spotlessly liveried mess staff, when we were surrounded by a group of goons. They sported extremely short, spiky haircuts that reminded me of the neo-Nazi cult, and acted as though they owned the place. The goons pounced on us as though they had been waiting for us to arrive. As we were bullied and harassed, a terrible thought flitted through my mind – if this was a precursor to my stay, spending six terms in the Academy would be a difficult proposition.

Official matters took precedence in the next few minutes. We were allotted our squadrons. I was told to report at the Golf (G) squadron, along with five others. The Academy comprised a total of twelve squadrons divided into three battalions of four squadrons each. These were identified by the alphabets from A to L, short for Alpha, Bravo, Charlie, Delta, Echo, Fox, Golf, Hunter, India, Juliet, Kilo and Lima.

A few of us were told to follow one of the seniors, on foot, to G squadron.

'Don't bother about the baggage; it will reach there,' we were assured.

Quickly, in my mind, I went through the list of things that the alphabet 'G' could denote. The letter stood for good, god, grand, great, glorious, and so on. It felt great to be a part of anything that began with the alphabet. But I was totally unprepared for what followed.

Two seniors greeted us at G squadron. 'Welcome to Gunda squadron,' they said. I was taken aback – not for a moment had any such negative association with the alphabet flitted through my mind.

The squadron was a three-storeyed stone structure. On each floor was a central corridor flanked by rooms on either side. Three staircases – one in the centre, and two at either end – led to each floor. A parade ground stood at the entrance of the squadron. We entered the squadron through the back door and lined up in the central corridor at the entrance. I looked reverently at the squadron that was to be my home for the next three years.

By this time, the vehicle with our luggage had also arrived at the parade ground in front of the squadron.

'Unload your belongings,' roared one of the seniors, and we scrambled to get our baggage out of the truck.

Barking seemed to be the prime qualification of the seniors. They barked at us for no reason: for not standing straight, for not addressing them as 'sir', for not looking straight, and also for not knowing their names or who they were. How the hell were we supposed to know their names, I wondered. Besides, everyone looked the same, with their hallmark cropped hair and vicious expression. The entire exercise of finding fault was an introduction to the fact that they were the masters, and we, the slaves.

All through the morning, none of us had exchanged a word, save trying a few tentative encouraging smiles. There was an element of fear, uncertainty, and nervousness that dominated the hearts of all the newcomers. Expect the unexpected, a wise guy had told me when I began my journey to Poona. The words seemed prophetic in the present context.

The goons set about trying to find enough reasons to punish us.

'You piddly chaps... don't know how to stand, and you want to join the NDA?'

'You there,' one of them ticked me off. 'Don't steal furtive glances like a convict, look straight ahead.'

According to them, anything and everything was wrong with the newcomers. Having found enough fault with us, they meted out punishments. Not a single guy was spared.

The entrance corridor was covered with a six-feet wide coir mat running a length of about thirty metres. We were told to get under the mat from one end, and emerge from the other. On the face of it, the punishment seemed simple enough. It was only after we had got under the mat that realization struck. There was enough dust accumulated under the mats to merit a storm. It choked our lungs, and stung the eyes; and the heat was unbearable. We sweated, spluttered, and crept ahead. I attempted snatching some fresh air by lifting a corner of the mat. The action brought an instant reaction in the form of a boot from a senior, which landed painfully on my arm. A sharp intake of breath drew in some more dust into my trachea, making me splutter. Bonfires erupted inside the cranium, and my stomach became a lava pit. All it needed was the water flowing out in rivulets from the eyes.

I closed my eyes and fought my way through the black hole, emerging gasping at the other end, clothes and face blackened beyond recognition. I could have easily impersonated a warrior from the deep jungles of Africa.

Satisfied by our performance, the seniors decided that it was time for allocation of rooms. Each squadron has about 125 rooms, with common bathrooms at either end of the corridor, on each floor. The first-termers were allotted rooms on the ground floor. A collective sigh of relief went down the line.

Now I can bathe and relax for a while, I thought. After all the muck I had loaded myself with, the idea of a bath seemed enticing.

Tentatively, I peeped into the cabin allotted to me, (rooms are called cabins in the Academy). It was about ten by ten feet, and had a single window with a shutter. Above the door was a strong wire mesh about three square inches, overlooking the corridor, for ventilation. For furniture we had a bed with a mattress, a study chair and a table, an easy chair, and a chest of drawers with a mirror on top. It seemed adequate enough.

I lugged my baggage to the room, glad that I had some privacy. At least we didn't have to share a room. Quickly, I shoved the trunk under the bed, unrolled the bedding on the bed, bolted the door, and flung myself on the bed. I was so exhausted that I didn't even pause to remove my shoes. In an instant I fell into a state of heavy, dreamless sleep.

'Pay attention, Golf squadron. All first-termers, report to the ground floor centre lobby immediately!' The announcement floated through my comatose brain, rudely trespassing on my slumber.

It took me a while to find my bearings. I decided to ignore the announcement. *Come on, it's just fair that a guy should have at least an hour's nap after all that he's gone through,* I muttered. I was answered by a thunderous kick that shook my door threateningly. I sprang out of the bed, and rushed outside, finger-combing my hair to settle it into a semblance of neatness.

I was late by a few seconds. A senior was waiting in the corridor to pounce on me. He smirked ominously as I screeched to a halt beside him and stood ramrod straight, staring at a fixed point ahead. It was a flawless copy of a posture I had noted in one of the Hollywood war movies. It failed, however, to impress the senior. Minutes later, I made a spectacular entry front-rolling all the way to the centre lobby.

Nine first-termers stood in a line. I noticed that the ones who had arrived before me sported the barber's delight, a 0.5-centimetre haircut. Surreptitiously, I fingered my long locks. The cadet sergeant major (CSM) barked, 'I want you back here after a bath, and change, in two minutes. Your time starts now.'

The guy must have been practising for a game show.

He is mad, I thought. It would not take less than half an hour to clean my soot-black self.

A flurry of arms and legs followed his announcement. We sprinted to our rooms to grab our towels, and ran towards the bathrooms at the end of the corridor. More surprise awaited us. The bathroom had no stalls. It was a large hall with a series of showers stuck on its tiled wall.

A cadet stood totally naked under the third shower. The only thing covered was his face, under a thick lather of soap. In the buff, there was no way of identifying if he was a senior. Surprised, I stared at him.

'What are you staring at?' he barked. 'Don't you have one, or do you have a hole instead? Strip, you prick!'

I had no choice in the matter. Time was running out, anyway. With my eyes closed, I peeled off my clothes, and rushed under a shower. The first time is the toughest, as they say. A snigger from my neighbour accelerated my bath. At the last count, there were ten more nude bodies under the showers in various postures. The lukewarm water felt heavenly, and I began to enjoy myself as I washed away all the dirt, along with the fatigue. The joy was short-lived as I remembered the two-minute deadline and raced back to my cabin, wrapped in a towel.

The seniors were monitoring our moves closely. Like the Gestapo, they paraded outside our rooms, the echo of their boots sending waves of fear through the first-termers. A kick or a knock on the door almost every second, kept us on our toes, and I emerged out of my room, after four minutes, sans watch, wallet, and handkerchief, with trailing shoelaces. Despite my record performance, I was two minutes behind the impossible deadline.

There were five first-termers already front-rolling from one end of the corridor to the other. Like huge balls of human limbs, they moved down the passageway, their roll accompanied by silent curses and muted groans. Without a word, I joined them. One lesson I had already learnt was not to question anyone, and front-rolling was the most popular punishment meted out to the first-termers.

A deluge of abuses rained from the seniors.

'Get off your arses!' shouted one of them. 'It is time for some modelling.'

While I was wondering what kind of modelling we were supposed to do, we were told to change into the games dress.

'And you get one minute for your feat,' the fellow bellowed.

Sadists, I thought. One minute – as though a war had broken out. We ducked into our rooms, and struggled with the shorts, shirt, and shoes and socks, all white. The laces seemed to elude my trembling fingers, despite my best efforts. I counted to ten and breathed deeply to control my rising stress level, and tried again.

Feat achieved, I ran back. Sure enough, it was more than one minute, and we began front-rolling again. I must admit that the punishment succeeded in turning us into humble souls. Kissing mother earth had not been an activity I had previously experienced. Besides, it helped in strengthening the spine, I told myself, trying to be positive about the entire exercise.

We had hardly assumed an upright position and stretched our tortured backs, when the next command came. 'Change into your PT dress and report here in thirty seconds.'

Every chap around knew that it was impossible to do so in the time granted by them. So it was just an excuse to punish us again. After that, it was the mufti (civil dress), and the battle order dress, and so on... with the time limit decreasing each time. We kept rolling till the entire world began spinning before our eyes. I was tempted to tell our tormentors that they could skip the orders and keep us rolling all day.

The guys were stark, raving lunatics. I cursed the day I had decided to put myself at their mercy. There must be something more to the training than the agony of punishments.

The charade continued for some time. Later, I learnt that this exercise of changing into different dresses in limited time was called 'Puttie Parade', and it was one of the favourite punishments of the seniors. This was one parade that needed to be mastered if one was to escape their ire. I also learnt that in the Academy, everything was a parade. There was the drill parade, PT (physical training) parade, outdoor parade, and umpteen others.

The exercise wasn't a total failure. I learnt to drop my pants faster than I had ever done.

At the end of the parade, my room looked as though a tornado had passed through it. With the dresses strewn all over the place, it was a royal mess. It seemed ages since I had landed in Poona, but I discovered that it was only about 11.00 a.m. We had accomplished a lot with nothing but perspiration to vouch for it.

'Now that you know what Puttie Parade is all about...,' said one of our tormentors dramatically, and paused for effect. If he was waiting for applause, he was wasting his time; none of us obliged him with even a smile. Then he said, 'It is time for you guys to get on to the seventh heaven.'

That sounded good. I sort of looked forward to the seventh heaven, a delicious sense of anticipation flooding my body. It had to be some sort of a treat or reward for all the punishment we had suffered.

'There, you see the wire mesh on your ventilator?' He pointed at the thick and jagged wire mesh over the door. 'Just hang on to it for your dear life.'

I was still gaping at it when a strong kick on the rear propelled me forward.

I finally deduced that the name 'seventh heaven' had originated because we had to hang from the seventh horizontal wire of the mesh.

The cry burst forth before I could suppress it. The torture of hanging from the sharp-edged wire, with my body weight dragging me down, was unimaginable. If this was the seventh heaven, give me hell any day. The wires cut into my fingers, and I wondered when I had last taken a tetanus shot. It was worse than a toothache, which I thought was most difficult to bear. In those agonizing moments, I remembered my father's warning about joining the Academy and for the first time, I wished I had heeded his advice.

Fortunately, it was time for our visit to the Quarter Master Store, so the ordeal ended earlier than expected.

TWO

Reluctantly, the seniors handed us over to an ustaad (an instructor from the non-officer ranks) assigned to break newcomers in who arrived at dot 11.00 a.m. to take us to issue our kits. Sighing with relief, we trailed him like the rats of Hamlin. We were taken to a small fort-like structure called the Quarter Master Fort, and issued with a whole lot of items like uniforms, and a robe, which would turn out to be the most sought-after attire, eventually. There were boots, socks, belts, caps, berets, towels, army packs and battle kit – quite a load.

For the first time since our arrival, we first-termers exchanged notes while we waited for our turn. We met cadets from other squadrons who had come with their ustaads. Like frogs that had slipped out of the serpents' mouths, we celebrated our brief period of liberation. All of us busied ourselves by sizing up each other I sucked in my breath and stood tall. No point in giving a bad impression; first impressions count. Aware that I had drawn a short stick when God was doling out beauty, the only thing I could take pride in was my proud and stately bearing, which I had practised a great deal before coming to NDA. With a bulbous nose and drooping eyes, I couldn't lay claim to comeliness, anyway.

I noticed the stocky fellow with a friendly face and curly hair, who had been allotted an adjoining cabin, and approached him. His eyes twinkled with suppressed mirth and his smile was infectious.

'Hi, I am Nikhil,' I extended my hand.

'Rebello. Albert Rebello,' he replied, pumping my hand with gusto. 'Remember me as Rebello, the rebel. That is what my schoolmates named me. You can call me Bertie.'

I was happy to have made one friend, and a jolly one at that. We could use some laughter here.

Randhir Singh, a tall and handsome Rajput, looked as though he had been poured into the uniform. He sauntered up to us, and suggested that we should stick together since we occupied neighbouring cabins. It sounded like a good idea. If we were to share things, thoughts, and punishments, the easiest chaps to share them with would be the ones staying next door.

We had barely introduced ourselves when a thin fellow with a hungry look approached us. Contrasted with Randhir's impeccable smartness, this guy's uniform looked as though it had been made for someone a tad bigger in size. His torso ended in a long neck that signalled gene mingling with a giraffe at some stage. It would have got a woman some crown in a beauty contest, but on him, it looked ludicrous. 'The name is Mitra. Manoj Mitra,' he grinned. 'You guys are next door, I noticed.'

The ice broken, we gave vent to our ire against the seniors. 'Watch it, guys. One of these days, I am going to extract every bit of revenge from those morons,' said Mitra, his face lighting up with anticipation.

Manoj was from Sainik School, Purulia. They teach you a lot of survival tricks at those schools that we, from the public schools, never learn. The mean look on his face assured me that he would keep his word.

The four of us were in neighbouring cabins and that helped in cementing our friendship.

Nath, a shy, diminutive fellow with appealing eyes completed our gang. Gifted with a baby face and ruddy cheeks, he looked younger than the others. Just over five feet, the roly-poly look added to his vulnerable little-boy-lost appearance. The only distinctive feature about Nath was his prominent Adam's apple, which had a way of bobbing up and down furiously at times of emotional upheaval. His cabin was at the other end of the passage, but he wanted to be in our company, anyway.

We laughed, backslapped and bantered while collecting our things, and lingered on as long as possible. No one wanted to get back to the squadron. The knowledge that the seniors were lying in wait for our return made us drag our feet. But all good things end, and the kit issue ended, too.

Our arms loaded, we finally returned to the cabins and dumped the lot. Arranging the mess in the cabin was out of question. There was just no time for that.

Minutes after our return to the squadron, we were told to line up at the barber's. A keen observer would certainly have noticed a likeness of facial expressions between us akin to sentenced convicts proceeding towards the gallows. The NDA haircut was not a popular style, to say the least.

'While you guys are getting your styling done, I might as well snatch a couple of winks,' laughed Harjinder Singh, a strapping Sikh with a dimpled smile. His remark was designed to sprinkle salt on our wounded hearts.

As I subjected my lovely locks to the heartless barbers, the most awful thought that passed through my mind was how I would face my folks back home. With the half-centimetre hairstyle, I would certainly be the epicentre of all jokes among friends! It took under two minutes of expert wielding of the scissors to demolish the six inches that had taken six months of loving care to grow. I stared, horrified, at my reflection. I was almost bald. My own mom could not have recognized me.

Aghast, we stared at each other. We all looked the same. The identical 'gobri' or 'katori' cut had managed to erase our individuality totally.

By now we were a ravenous lot. A bath later, accompanied by a fifth-term sergeant, we ran all the way to the mess for lunch. It was another one of those unjust writs of the Academy that no first-termer was allowed to walk. We had to run everywhere in proper formation. Other first-termers from different squadrons had also begun trickling into the dining hall.

The mess was huge, fringed with well-kept lawns and a derelict aircraft was placed right in front of the building. The dining hall reminded me of Hollywood epoch movies. Like an immense banquet hall, it was designed to seat over 1500 people, and the ambience was very formal.

We were assigned seats that were to be our permanent place for all meals. Patrick was the first person from the Academy who displayed a kindly disposition. His face beaming, the portly fellow with touches of grey in his hair, had the unenviable task of catering for a famished pack of first-termers. He was like a mother hen, doling out cheer and dishes to the newcomers, which did a lot to boost our sagging morale. We attacked food like freeloaders at a wedding party.

The sergeant's growl slowed us down and reminded us of our surroundings. 'Pigs! Where are your table manners?' he screamed, drowning the din of the spoons and forks which were attacking the plates ruthlessly.

We slowed down for a few minutes before accelerating our jaw movement to 120 rounds per minute, once again. I lost count of the number of helpings I took of each dish. Food had never tasted more delicious.

Tongues finally loosened on our way back to the squadron. A

full belly has a way of making the most harassed of people careless. Instinctively, the four of us – Mitra, Rebello, Randhir and I – fell together. We kept our voices low, trying to talk while on the run. Running after a huge meal was neither agreeable nor good for digestion. A few farts from the front told us so.

Mitra lamented the absence of fish in the meal. He couldn't survive without fish, he confided. 'It makes my brain cells work better.' His predilection for the dish reminded me of Bertie Wooster, and I had to bite my tongue to stop a wisecrack.

'I could do with some butter chicken,' remarked Rebello. We were to learn that his life depended on chicks of all kinds.

'And I, with some siesta,' Randhir and I spoke together.

All wishful thoughts of a siesta after the heavy meal evaporated as soon as we reached the squadron. A senior sporting cauliflower ears arrived importantly, and announced that the afternoon was reserved for issuing bikes. In the NDA, a bike is the only means of commuting for the cadets, and possessing it ensured that we saved our energy as well as time.

'At least we won't have to run from place to place like prehistoric creatures,' opined Bertie.

The bicycles came with the squadron name, and the bike number marked on the rear mudguard. I thumped mine appreciatively. The maintenance of the bike was our responsibility, we were informed by the ustaad.

Nath was the only one who didn't seem particularly pleased with his bike. After spending some time fingering the contraption, he sighed loudly a couple of times. He looked more and more depressed as he lugged his bike to the squadron.

We had scarcely parked the bikes when a senior informed us that it was time for the 'Cabin Cupboard' parade.

'What's that?' we wondered.

'Couldn't be a punishment I am sure,' remarked Mitra.

He couldn't have been farther from the truth.

In simple terms, 'Cabin Cupboard' meant organizing our rooms to a set layout.

We were taken to a room and shown a demo layout.

'There should be no deviation,' said the sixth-termer, with a voice like a peacock crying for rain. All that screaming and shouting at the juniors must have done the trick, I concluded. With a rasping voice like that, he couldn't be ignored.

'Everything should be placed just as displayed. You don't have the liberty to exercise your interior decoration talents.'

'Any doubts?' The chap with the peacock voice threw us a threatening look. 'You have twenty minutes to set your rooms,' he ended.

'By Jove,' lamented Bertie in an undertone. 'Twenty minutes for a job that will not take less than an hour!'

'Put all your junk in the black steel trunk. There should not be a speck of dust anywhere. All items in the cabin must be cleaned and folded.' More instructions streamed out of the senior's mouth.

I stared ruefully at my room. It looked as though a clumsy robber had gone through it, with clothes strewn all over the place, shoes flung along the walls their laces knotted; berets, belts and socks occupying a major part of the floor and bed. The Puttie Parade, with its umpteen dress changes in limited time, had turned the cabin into a dumping ground. There was no way I could create a semblance of order. Wistfully, I thought of my mother who had spared the rod and spoilt her child, as I went to work.

'Stop working and stand outside your room!' an announcement encroached upon my attention precisely after twenty minutes. I quickly darted out of the room and stood ramrod straight outside my door.

The sergeant began his inspection. He entered the first cabin, and we heard a lot of shouting and banging, and the next instant, all the possessions were flying out of the room and landing into the corridor. Seconds later, a crestfallen cadet emerged from the cabin, looking numb with disbelief. In two minutes, the sergeant had demolished his twenty-minutes' labour. The same exercise was repeated in all the other rooms.

'You morons, get your act together! The next inspection will take place in half an hour.'

Was there an award for ruthlessness, the sergeant was sure to bag it.

A hectic thirty minutes later, I took a step back and admired my handiwork. Every object in the room was in the right place, neatly arranged. *Even he won't be able to find any fault now, I thought smugly.*

It is amazing how quickly smugness can be wiped off from a face.

The brute entered my room and threw me a blistering glance, after which he went on to pore over shoelaces and mosquito-net poles, and peeped under the bed where I had cramped many assorted belongings, just as I had seen my mother do when we had unexpected guests.

'The shoelaces are twisted, and look at all this dust.' The sergeant announced, running his finger on the mosquito-net poles. The temperature in the room had dipped by at least ten degrees, and I shivered. 'You call this cleaning?'

My right eye flickered ominously as he strutted around hunting for more flaws. When he stood on his toes and ran his index finger along the top of the door, I resisted an urge to jump out of the window. Grinning rather unpleasantly, he displayed his grimy finger and wiped it across my face. 'Next time, I will make you lick it clean,' he said. His impersonation of a Bollywood villain was perfect.

With his excellence at nit-picking, the sergeant could have cleaned up the heavily infested scalp of a baboon in five minutes flat. The clothes were not folded properly, the shoes not lined up correctly. The bed, chair, and tables, were not aligned. In short, everything was wrong with the room.

He chucked my possessions around the room mercilessly, and allotted a new deadline for me to tidy up once again. A diabolical smile lit up his face each time he entered the room. Six times I did up the cabin, and six times he emerged triumphantly from it, having found innumerable faults. By then, my head was spinning rather perilously.

Cabin Cupboard continued till tea-time. If I thought tea would be a pleasant affair, I was mistaken.

Each squadron had a tearoom on the first floor corridor. The room was equipped with a huge boiler. Come tea-time, and a waiter from the mess arrived with a huge tray laden with snacks and the tea-making paraphernalia. The cadet quarter master sergeant's (CQMS) room stood right across the tearoom. It was here that the snacks were brought and counted. The rules set by the seniors were quite simple:

Rule 1: If a senior decided to have more than his share of snacks, it came from a first-termer's share.

Rule 2: Seniors never went to get their tea; the first-termers brought it to them.

Rule 3: The seniors had their favourite mugs. Breaking them was blasphemous and could take you to the seventh heaven.

Tea-time was the worst time for the first-termers. It was the time when the squadron was in full strength and there was utter chaos. With so many seniors around, we were hard pressed to serve them on time, and more importantly, to their satisfaction.

That evening, I had to carry nine mugs of tea for the seniors. Naturally, I could not remember their names, cabin numbers, faces and terms, and above all, the identity of the mug owners. It was a good exercise for the brain. I could well imagine the plight of the chokra (boy) waiters in small restaurants jam-packed with customers.

The tea was boiling hot, and the mugs scalding. My fingers were almost blistered with the effort of dispensing the brew. All the first-termers were suffering the same plight and many spilled the tea, causing minor accidents. The only positive thing about the exercise was that we were getting trained for an alternative career, should we decide to quit the army prematurely.

To add insult to our injuries, the rascals left no snacks for us.

It was party time in the CQMS's room where the sixth-termers assembled and pigged on the snacks meant for us. We were issued with enamelled mugs, which could hold almost a litre of tea, and there was no restriction on the amount one could pour down the gullet. After all the slogging, even the terribly concocted tea tasted divine.

'One of these days I am going to pour boiling tea on the CQMS's crotch,' declared Mitra wickedly. For the moment, we satisfied ourselves conjuring up the image of the chap hopping around with burnt genitals.

My hands cupped around the mug, I was dreaming of the things I would do to extract revenge when I was called by CSM (cadet sergeant major) and asked to make an announcement.

'Pay attention Golf squadron! All first-termers to report to the ante-room at 5.00 p.m. sharp!' I yelled, mimicking the CSM, feeling like a hero. In that instant also dawned the realization of the power one enjoyed while yelling out a command. No wonder the chaps were always on a high.

It was already 4.45 p.m., and we had no clue about the location of the anteroom. When I dared to put forth the collective query before the CSM, I was made to execute a couple of front rolls.

'That will teach you not to ask questions – that is our prerogative!' he roared. 'I want you to have a bath, and then report at the anteroom by 5.00 p.m..'

The information that the anteroom was at the end of the ground floor corridor came to me the hard way. By now, I had resigned myself to the fact that whatever we did would always be wrong, and endless punishments were our ultimate fate. One didn't question God.

I sprinted back to my room. A bath was something that I really needed after the grime that had accumulated during the hectic schedule and the haircut. It wasn't just the dirt; the smell of perspiration from my body would have shamed a skunk.

Sometimes in life, we have to satisfy ourselves with small achievements. This was definitely one of those times. I achieved a bath and a change of clothes within record time. My sprinting feet skidded to a throbbing halt near the anteroom just in time to join the last of the first-termers trooping in.

The anteroom was a hub of activity as we settled in and soaked in the ambience. It was tastefully decorated with mementos gifted by each batch of cadets that had passed out from the Academy. With its aquarium, a promising-looking music system, comfortable sofas and luxurious ambience, it was a comforting haven.

Seventeen first-termers were seated on the floor. I joined Mitra and Rebello, and we wondered what lay ahead.

'Must be another of their crackpot ideas leading to some more punishment,' Mitra declared resignedly.

'My fingers are bent with all that climbing I have done to reach heaven,' said Rebello, examining them thoughtfully. 'And the front-rolling makes me see stars all the time,' he added, blinking his eyes to endorse the fact.

'And you thought training for the army was child's play?' Randy's voice sounded sarcastic.

Natty chuckled timidly. 'It is like a replay of the SS troops and their Jew captives.'

Just as the suspense began to kill us, the fifth-term sergeant arrived. A hush fell over our lot as he briefed us about the schedule for the next day. A moment later, two bigwigs, the SCC (squadron cadet captain), and the CSM, marched into the room. Compared to the pompous CSM, the SCC appeared like an angel who had lost his way into the Academy. The greenhorns we were, we got taken in by his courtesy. He began by asking us if we were comfortable and happy, if the food was good, and if we had any problems. '*Happy! He's got to be joking,*' muttered Rebello under his breath.

All of us were dying to complain about the CSM who kept us on our feet and made us do inhuman things, but we held our tongue. By now, we had learnt not to push our luck too far.

It was time for formal introductions. We parroted details about our family, our academic qualifications, hobbies, the games we enjoyed playing, and other irrelevant things he asked us about. I had no doubt that he wasn't even listening, but the exercise provided us with an opportunity to learn the names of our course mates, and get to know a little about them.

Manoj Mitra, I learnt, was the son of a bank officer, with a younger sister who was his alter ego. His dream, he said, had been to become a chef in a five-star hotel, but his father wished otherwise. For hobbies, he listed eating fish and appreciating the taste. We wondered how his smart alec act would go down with the seniors, but for the moment, they seemed to tolerate him. The retribution would come later.

That very instant, Rebello granted him a perfect name, Maachh (which means 'fish' in Bengali). The moniker would stick to him for the rest of his life.

Albert Rebello (Bertie), the youngest of three sons, belonged to a seafood business family in Goa. This information perked up Mitra's flagging attention, and he promptly decided to visit Rebello's folks at the first possible opportunity.

Getting back to Bertie's kin, his eldest brother helped in the business, while the next one studied medicine. Rebello was the good-for-nothing black sheep, and had been sent to Lovedale School, Ooty, so that he could get disciplined. At school, he proved himself adept with musical instruments and a master of pranks.

Obsessed with aircraft, it was his idea to join the NDA because he wanted to be a pilot in the air force.

Randhir Singh (Randy), from the land of valiant Rajputs, belonged to a family of soldiers. His father was a distinguished Sena Medal holder, and all his elder brothers were in the army. With a background like that, he had no option but to join the armed forces.

Amar Nath (Natty) was the midget. Just over five feet three inches, he was the guy with a dimpled smile from the hills of Haldwani. With four sons and two daughters, his parents struggled to make ends meet on the salary his father brought home as a schoolteacher. Joining the NDA was the most affordable option, and so, here he was. Absolutely uncorrupted, the guy was a sucker for all sob stories. He loved movies as much as he loved the hills.

I skipped unsavoury details about myself and shared only the barest information. All I told them was that I was the youngest of three brothers, with two sisters at either end – a large family by all means. I couldn't tell the gathering that I had joined the NDA against the wishes of my parents. My father, who was a doctor, had threatened to remove my name from the family annals because I had defied him to appear for the selection test. The fact that I had concealed my selection in the Academy till the last date went against me and negated any good deeds performed earlier. My mother had used her most lethal arsenal – copious tears – to deter me from coming to Poona.

Once we had finished the introductions, the SCC asked if we had written to our parents or spoken to them. He reminded us that we should do so immediately unless we wanted our mothers descending upon the Academy. A few forced giggles intended to please the chap poured in from all directions, and the meeting was declared over.

The first person to leave the anteroom was the SCC. All hell broke loose within a moment of his departure. The CSM got after us almost immediately. He ordered us out in the corridor, and made us front-roll all along its length. His reasons were as absurd as Hitler's reasons for decimating the Jews: we did not sit straight, our backs bent like old hags, we were not officer material, and our posture was totally unfit for a cadet. He looked at us with disgust, as though we were some slugs that had just crawled out from under a boulder.

'I guess you need to roll some more,' was his final verdict.

We kept front-rolling while the sixth-termers gathered in the CSM's room. We could hear loud laughter and banter.

'Wretched lunatics,' muttered Maachh. 'They must have escaped from a sanatorium.'

'I guess we can take a break,' said Rebello. 'They are too busy sharing jokes to pay any attention to us.'

We stopped rolling and relaxed. But the CSM was an experienced chap. He peeped out of his room at regular intervals and caught some cadet or the other, and made him climb the seventh heaven. The punishment carried on for an hour till it was dinner-time.

We were a sight as we ran towards the mess for dinner, exhausted, dishevelled and sweaty. The notions I harboured about the lunacy of the seniors from our squadron were dispelled the moment I spotted our counterparts from other squadrons arriving in the same state, if not worse. It took all of Patrick's broad smiles and the piping hot food to soothe our ruffled feathers and put us in a better frame of mind.

Perhaps it was our fatigue and hunger that made the meal more delicious. Basically, it was quantity and not quality that mattered. Right from the soup to the dessert, we took more than one serving of everything. For once, even Maachh did not crib about the absence of fish from the menu.

His mood improved when a couple of sixth-termers from another squadron came over to our table and spoke to him. These guys were also from Sainik School, Purulia, Maachh's alma mater. Raghubir, another first-termer, also found some seniors who were from his school.

After dinner we went back to the squadron minus Maachh and Raghubir, who had accompanied the seniors to their squadrons. The moment we reached the squadron and assembled in front of the CSM's cabin, we were subjected to another lecture from the chap. The guy loved nothing better than his voice, we surmised.

After sermonizing to us for a few minutes, he noticed that Maachh and Raghubir were missing. We thought he would have a fit the way he hopped with anger when he learnt that they had gone with some sixth-termers.

'Some of you might think it is smart to tag along with a senior,' he said, almost frothing at the mouth. 'Let me warn you that those who take lift from the seniors have just had it.'

'Taking lift' in this case meant taking advantage of the relationship with seniors from other squadrons. 'Just you wait and watch. I will make specimens out of those two guys,' the CSM warned.

Just then, Maachh and Raghubir arrived, grinning from ear to ear. The duo seemed quite pleased with life as they strolled in casually. The CSM subjected them to a deadly stare before announcing icily, 'Here come the VIPs of our squadron.'

Unsuspecting, the two continued to smile beatifically till they heard the next sentence, 'The VIPs deserve special treatment, and I am going to give it to them, now.'

Then began a series of punishments for the two, while we stood silently and watched. They were subjected to Puttie Parade, seventh heaven, and front-rolling, everything the frustrated CSM could think of. Maachh was made to go down on his hands, and Raghubir was made to lift his legs and push him forward like a wheelbarrow. Then they were told to reverse roles. This continued for quite some time. All this was too much for Raghubir to bear after the heavy dinner, and he began to vomit. That put an end to the punishment and we were finally let off at about 11.00 p.m. Too tired for anything else, I collapsed into a dreamless slumber moments before my head touched the pillow.

THREE

At 4.30 a.m., we woke up to a loud announcement in a first-termer's quivering voice, 'All first-termers double down to the ground floor centre lobby.'

He had been instructed the previous evening to make the announcement at dot 4.30 a.m. Yawning, and rubbing the sleep out of our eyes, we rushed down, pulling our robes on. It was still dark, and the only light reflected anxious and drowsy faces. Finding that none of the seniors had come down, we began to relax and chat with each other.

Decibels rose as the tension ebbed, and soon we were in the backslapping stage of advanced camaraderie. A little later, the CSM emerged, swinging his arms and legs importantly. He glanced at us in a menacing manner and hurled abuses for waking him up at the unearthly hour, conveniently forgetting the fact that it was he who had instructed us to assemble there at 4.30 a.m.

He was as grouchy as a bear with toothache and now that he was up, he was in a mood to settle scores with us. Our Academy haircut provided him with no opportunity to inspect our hair, so he started checking our beards.

'How many of you shave?' he asked.

A solitary hand went up. This did not please the CSM, who, in any case, was looking for excuses to pick on us.

Rahul was first in the line. He was probably just sixteen.

'You idiot, come here! Do you shave?' he asked.

'No, sir.'

'Why?'

The CSM searched his face intently, and after much hunting, he pulled out a single hair from his chin and demanded, 'What is this, you skunk? Go and shave. You have one minute.'

It was my turn next. He peered short-sightedly at my smooth cheeks, in the semi-darkness. Frustrated that the search didn't yield the desired results, he ordered Sameer to fetch a torch. My heart pounded loudly. I had never shaved. Neither did I own a shaving kit. The torch beam also failed to light up any significant growth on the chin.

Not ready to accept defeat, the CSM concluded, 'You are now half a man. To become a complete man, you have to shave.' He roared, 'Half a minute! I want you all back, shaved and clean'.

A melee followed as all the half-men ran around for shaving kits. With hardly a couple of cadets possessing them, there was total chaos. Harjinder Singh, the surd (short for 'sardar'), was the only guy who looked unperturbed. After a frantic search, a couple of razors were located, and all of us tried our best to cope. That was the first time I shaved, and my face was full of nicks and cuts. *Half a minute, goddamnit*! I nicked some more. In any case, with no facial hair, there was only the skin to scrape. My face was a burning mass of skin that stung with each splash of cold water on it.

Relief came in the form of a sumptuous breakfast. The dining room was the only haven for the first-termers, who sought to bury their frustration in the food-filled platters. Unlike the other hostels, food in the Academy was good and plentiful. It sort of compensated for our suffering.

After breakfast, the washerman arrived with our uniforms that were starched and ironed to perfect stiffness. Raju, the orderly, was a veteran. He was assigned eight first-termers. His job was to keep all the uniforms in the proper places, shoes and belts polished, and the brass fixed on the uniforms, which were to be worn for the drill the next morning. Brass badges with the squadron 'G' and our term '1' were fixed on the collar. The uniform also had the insignia and the crest of the NDA, along with a nameplate. All these had to be constantly kept in sparkling state.

Raju warned us not to touch the uniform or wear it till he arrived in the morning. The crease was not to be broken at any cost, he cautioned.

By noon, the NDA special – a special train for cadets from Delhi to Poona – had arrived. The squadron was swarming with cadets from different terms. It was the ultimate test for the first-termers. More seniors meant more trouble. Right from the second- to sixth-termers, everyone was a boss. To add to our problems, we had no way of knowing who was from the second term and who belonged to the sixth.

With the signature haircuts, lean frames, and arrogant stance, they all looked alike. It would take a genius to remember the names, terms, and cabins, and we definitely didn't belong to that genre.

Being at the bottom of the ladder is terribly injurious to health, we realized, as we transformed into coolies for the next few hours. As each bus arrived with a fresh batch of cadets, and trucks with their baggage, we were kept busy hauling their belongings to their cabins. Utter pandemonium reigned over the squadron. If we were running an errand for a second-termer, a third-termer would hijack us. The only first-termers who couldn't be touched by the others were the ones who were running an errand for a sixth-termer.

I was running from floor to floor, ordered about by a different set of slave-drivers. Sweat ran down my back as I struggled with the heavy boxes, while my spine threatened to deform itself forever. Then I spotted Harry, another first-termer, lolling by the staircase.

'Hey, bigwig,' I called, 'How come you are enjoying yourself while all of us are running around like monkeys?'

'Correction, dear friend,' he ticked me off. 'Running like donkeys. Monkeys have more brains. You guys don't have any, so you are donkeys.'

'Cut the joke, Harry,' I warned. 'It isn't even funny.'

'Don't get angry, buddy. Use your brains,' he said, and strutted over to me, tapping his turban dramatically. 'All you have to do is to say that you are running an errand for a sixth-termer, and no one will touch you.'

A few minutes later, I joined him after I had sent some third-termers scurrying by claiming that I was running an errand for a sixthy.

At last it was lunchtime, and we sighed with relief as we ran up to the mess for lunch. Carrying the heavy metal trunks from the box room, cleaning and dusting the seniors' rooms had turned us into ravenous beasts. Dirty, dishevelled, with sweat running down our backs, we looked more like coolies than cadets.

We got an inkling of the real routine after lunch when the weekly programme was issued, and a timetable was pinned to the notice board.

Hours seemed to rush at a supersonic speed, and before we could catch our breath, it was tea-time. This was the time when the squadron was in full strength. Like in a Kumbh Mela, the cadets from all terms dashed around creating confusion. I spotted Maachh trying to pass off as a second-termer. It wasn't long before he was caught by an alert fifth-termer and punished for his charade. The next time I saw him, he was standing on his hands with his legs propped against the wall, his fair face ruddy. I shook my head and smiled. That guy never gave up trying.

Most of the cadets turned up in their games dress or robe, and had their tea in cabins or corridors, after which they had a bath, changed, and proceeded to the anteroom for briefing. It was a set schedule, and everyone seemed to know the agenda except the first-termers who looked as confused as pigs in a rooster party.

By the time we returned to our rooms at night, it was almost the witching hour. For a flash of a second I thought of home, and realized that I had not spoken to my parents or written a letter. I pulled out the inland letter form that my mom had given me at the last moment, and began penning a few lines, but before I could finish the first paragraph, I had fallen asleep.

The next morning was more hectic than the previous one, as the training began in real earnest. The flurry of activities had already begun when I got up. We had to line up (fall-in) at the squadron parade ground with our satchels and bikes, and proceed to the drill square.

Dressing up for the drill was a big pain; one could not dress on one's own. The crease had to remain razor-sharp while the dress was worn, and the shirt had to be absolutely taut over the torso. Any crease in either of the garments was likely to attract stiff punishment. Unlike in regular dressing, we started the process of dressing in drill uniform feet upwards, starting with the drill boots so that we didn't have to bend later. The khaki shorts and belt went next, and the shirt was the last thing to be worn.

After I had worn the shirt, Raju arrived. We all lined up, and he put his hands under each one's shorts and pulled the shirt to stretch it tight over our chests, while we stood ramrod straight. The sight of his hands disappearing under the shorts looked most obscene.

We walked like robots, straight and stiff, so that the crease would not wrinkle. The bikes had to be lugged too. We could not ride them to the parade ground for the same reason. Nath dragged his bike along, as he had a flat tyre. I noticed that he always seemed to have a flat.

'Bloody cadets,' the voice of our ustaad greeted us as we neared the venue. 'Double up.'

He inspected our dress, haircut, and every possible aspect of our appearance. It was agonizing to stand there while the inspection went on, but not a single cadet dared to move save for a twitch of the muscles. To earn the wrath of the ustaad was like committing hara-kiri, we had been warned by the experienced ones.

We had been told that the ustaad had enormous powers and he could punish us by allotting extra duties and drills. He checked us for 'loose belt' by trying to stick his hand inside the belt and tugging at it. If he succeeded in grabbing the belt, we would be punished for 'loose belt'. What most of us did was suck in our breaths and tighten the belt as much as possible just before we reached the drill square. In this breathless state we remained till the end of the drill, after which we promptly loosened the belt and let our lungs expand with the oxygen we breathed in greedily.

The ustaads were the best jawans the Indian army had produced, and they were very capable. The only sore point was their inadequate grasp over the Queen's language. Those who could speak a smattering of English were assigned the job of teaching the foreign cadets, and it was a big high for them. This made them perfect targets for our jokes.

The charges the ustaads framed against the cadets were hilarious. A second-term cadet was once charged with 'dirty face' as he had not shaved properly. Another one was similarly charged for not brushing his teeth well.

We were horrified when we heard the story of the third-termer who had been charged for being 'naked on parade' by an ustaad. How could the imbecile have turned up naked for a parade? The shocked look on our faces was enough to send the narrator into peals of laughter.

'Don't let your imagination go haywire; the chap didn't really turn up naked. He just had a hobnail missing from his boots.' He chuckled. 'There are thirteen hobnails on the drill boots, and even a single one missing could lead to the charge of being "naked on parade".'

There was another one about a cadet who in a hurry to report for the drill, had not only forgotten the rifle but also forgotten to button up his fly. The missing rifle went unnoticed and the cadet got away with a light punishment for the open fly buttons. All those jokes came flooding back to my mind as I stood ramrod straight, but dared not let even a hint of a smile cross my features. I didn't want to be charged for being a 'funny face'.

Once the inspection was over, the drill began in real earnest. It was nothing but banging the feet with full force on the ground, the objective being to generate the maximum din one could manage. Each time we banged the foot down hard on the concrete, our brains seemed to wobble within the confines of our skulls. Pleasing the ustaad was mandatory if we had to escape punishment.

'I will catch you for B,' was his threat. The 'B' in this instance could be anything that began with the alphabet 'B' – beret, belt, buckle, brass, boot or even 'baal' (hair).

It was sheer blackmail, and there was no choice in the matter. The enormous leather boots we had to wear were very heavy with their thirteen hobnails, and the horseshoe fitted on the sole. Not just the head but also the body ached with the effort of banging our feet on the concrete.

It was a relief when the drill was over. It meant that we could ride the bicycle back to the mess although it also meant that we couldn't use the same dress set again till it was washed, starched and ironed. The drill always left us perspiring even in the severest of winter mornings.

'Boy, how would I love to put those guys through drills all day long,' wished Maachh, cycling along solemnly. 'My bloody brain seems to have been shaken out of its position.'

'No wonder my father always maintains that army men are all brawn and no brains,' I commented wryly.

'I love brawn, man. Brains, anyone can possess, but brawn requires a lot of stomping around on a drill ground,' Rebello added another of his funny lines. His funny one-liners were the only motivational force that saw us through all the suffering.

'What ails you my friend? You seem to have gone to hell and back twice over,' he ribbed Natty, who, as usual, was running with his bike. None of us had ever seen him riding it. 'Why don't you get your bike fixed?'

Ever since the bikes were issued, Natty had been displaying a morose expression, which varied just about a degree from the last one. His otherwise cheerful disposition seemed to have sunk into the depths of gloom for whatever reason. We presumed that he was missing his family. All the ragging and slogging must have got him down. Not once had he been spotted astride his bike.

'Is there something we can do?' I asked sympathetically.

'No, it's my funeral,' he replied tersely.

'Don't speak of funerals, dear chap. They remind me of my dead aunt,' Bertie thumped his back. 'Things can't be so dismal.'

'I guess it is his bike, the mother of all troubles,' Maachh said confidently. 'Look buddy, let us take it for repairs. I'll come with you,' he offered.

The sympathy showered on him from all sides touched a cord, and Nath broke down. 'It's not the bike,' he cried. 'It is just that I don't know how to ride one.'

His confession came like a bolt from the sky. Can anyone not know how to ride a bike? We were incredulous. Now we realized why his bike always had a flat. It was intentional.

Over the next three days, we took turns to teach Natty how to ride his bike. At the end of those three days, he just about managed to remain precariously poised on it. At the first hint of traffic, he lost his nerve and dismounted.

Each morning we woke up dreading the drill. If it was not drill, it would be PT, and PT meant sprinting, climbing ropes, doing pull ups on beams, jumping over wooden horses, and medicine ball – all kinds of gadgets invented to inflict torture on humankind. At times it was 'double outdoor' which was the mother of all pains. Double outdoor meant both drill and PT before breakfast. It was an infernal nuisance because we had to wear one dress while carrying the other.

For me, the gadgets were a novelty. Lucky to have escaped them until then, I was at total unease with the thingumajigs while the Sainik School products could work miracles on them. Even the lazy Maachh had an expertise that I openly envied. He could do obstacles, jumps, and function with absolute control while I tumbled over them continuously. My clumsiness manifested itself as vivid black and blue marks all over my body.

The ever-watchful eyes of the ustaads lighted up with a demonic gleam whenever they found a 'bakra' (scapegoat) like me. The slightest of errors drew severe punishments.

I got a taste of their sadistic tendency one morning when I could not climb the vertical rope the proper way (according to the ustaad's stipulation). In a flash, he was by my side. 'Nonsense, cadet!' he yelled. 'Up chadho, up chadho, jaldi, jaldi (Climb up, climb up, fast).'

When his 'up' was not achieved and I kept sliding down, it got too much for the guy. 'Theek hai,' he gritted his teeth. 'Up nahin ja sakta, to tham. Wahin theher (All right, if you can't climb up, halt, and remain stationary).'

Only a guy who has tried to remain static on a vertical rope knows that it is an impossible, gravity-defying exercise. There I was, hanging like an incapacitated baboon halfway up the rope, with the fiend lurking below. I kept sliding down and he whacked me each time I slid a few inches. To evade his thwack, I would move up a few inches and then slip down promptly. My hands and feet, scraped with the effort, had begun blistering. No doubt my feat appeared extremely hilarious to the onlookers, and I heard a few muffled chortles.

In the meantime, the grounds had witnessed a couple of casualties. I wasn't the only one who had injured his person as well as pride. As the hour drew to a close, there was a collection of cadets who wanted to report sick at the Medical Inspection (MI) Room; not just the injured ones.

It was all Natty's fault. He had been to the MI Room the previous day and come back raving about the young lady doctor who had attended to his wounds.

'She is too beautiful, yaar. Simply great. What a figure!' His eyes went berserk tracing the path of orbs.

'What is her name?' we enquired in one voice.

'Manisha Das.'

Based on Natty's information, the cadets began filtering into the MI Room, looking for the compassionate angel who would not only apply some balm to their wounds but also to their lacerated souls. The number of sick cadets swelled overnight, as though the Academy was in the grip of an unknown scourge. The slightest scratch was used as an excuse to land up at the MI Room.

Manisha, however, was a smart one. She had passed out from the Armed Forces Medical College (AFMC), Poona, and knew how to deal with greenhorns. She lined up the cadets who reported sick, and segregated the genuinely sick ones from the pretenders.

After that, she began doling out punishments instead of pills. The malingerers were given punishments like front-rolling and haunching. For additional effect, she threatened them with injections and enemas. After half an hour of punishments, they were asked how many wanted to report sick. Most of the cadets were happy to run back to their squadrons. A few brave ones who persisted, were made to strip and given enemas by the medical assistants. Word soon spread around and that was the end of sickness in the Academy. Everyone seemed to be blooming with good health, thereafter. Cadets with slight fever or small ailments resorted to self-treatment rather than report sick.

As luck would have it, during the very next PT period, I hurt my knee while vaulting over the wooden horse. The pain was terrible, and I limped into the MI Room. Since the injury was internal, Manisha could not spot any external signs and assumed that I was one of the malingerers.

'So, you have wounded your knee. That's bad,' she sized me up. 'I think you will be all right if you stood on your hands for a few hours.'

She wrote 'Excused legs', as the prescription for my ailment.

I was ordered to stand on my hands, head down and legs up against the wall. It was excruciatingly painful, but I could do little else than groan.

After about ten minutes, I told her that my knee didn't pain any more.

'That's very good,' she smiled. 'See, how easy it is to cure an injured knee?'

I cursed her. She had a stone inside the rib cage, a cold one at that. She was in the wrong profession, she should have been a butcher instead of a doc. I wondered if all army doctors were like her. It was better to attend drill and games, I decided, as I limped back to the squadron, than to be subjected to her sadistic ways.

FOUR

The rush back to the squadron after the outdoor activities, for a bath and change, would have set some kind of an Olympic record. Even the habitually slow cadets learnt to race with the rats. It wasn't just the cheese but the skin they were saving. We, the rats, raced on bikes on smooth roads instead of velodromes, at breakneck speed, heading for our respective squadrons. The problem was that we first-termers, being not so equal rats, had to ride in a formation or squad with ten, twelve or fourteen bikes in two rows, with one cadet in the front and one at the rear, the pace being set by the leader of the pack. As our rat contingent moved on the road, ustaads and sixth-term office holders lined up on both sides to ensure that no one broke the rules. The objective was to pick out the errant rat.

It was one of those days reserved for 'double outdoors' when life got spinning at double speed. As I explained earlier, double outdoors meant successive periods of drill and PT.

Time was at a premium, and rushing back towards the squadron, we rode our bikes at a super speed. As we were coming down the slope in front of the Sudan Block, Natty's brakes suddenly failed. The rubber brake shoes had come off, and the wheel rims emitted sparks when he braked hard. Confused at the unexpected fireworks, he looked down at the wheels, and in doing so, he broke the ranks. The ustaad began blowing his whistle frantically. Despite his best effort to bring the cycle to a halt, Natty lost control and banged it against a divider. He executed a neat front-roll with his bike and crashed into the bushes, which was a damn lucky thing, as the bushes cushioned his fall and he stood up without any injury.

The front-roll and the subsequent performance would have been impressive enough to extract a standing ovation elsewhere, but there, on the road, it managed to have us doubling up with laughter. It also spelt double trouble for poor Natty.

The ustaad yelled furiously, 'Nonsense cadet! Tu air force cadet hai kya? Cycle chalata hai ki jet? (Nonsense, cadet! Are you an air force cadet? Are you riding a cycle or a jet?).'

'Nonsense' was an oft-repeated prefix for the first-term cadets. The ustaads had a particular penchant for the word, I noticed. Poor Natty had to lift his bike above his head and double back to the squadron.

The double outdoors whipped up our appetite, and we rushed to the squadron for a bath, and then to the mess for breakfast. The two feats needed to be accomplished within an impossible deadline before we went for our theory classes.

A slow cadet had to skip his bath or breakfast. Missing either was impossible, so the only way out was to speed up one's life. At the rate our lives were spinning, I thought we could soon compete with the meteors.

Like a pack of hungry wolves, we attacked the fare Patrick put before us for breakfast. Most first-term cadets tucked in no less than two dozen toasts. But, like all other good things, the butter came in limited quantities. The toasts, of course, were unlimited, and so we acquired the art of eating six to ten toasts with 25 grams of butter, and an additional four to six toasts with a double-egg omelette. All of us were gluttons of the first order, but Maachh was an exceptional case. He ate like a starving python. It was amazing the amount of food he could put into his cavernous inside, and yet have nothing to show for it. His famished, Somalia-returned look remained intact.

Not all seniors were heartless. There were some who passed down their share of butter to the first-termers. There couldn't have been a better way to earn respect from the hungry lot of first-term cadets.

With our stomachs sated, it was time to exercise our brain cells. Reluctantly, we moved on to the Sudan Block and the Science Block for classes. The Sudan Block was for non-science subjects, and the Science Block for the sciences.

The syllabus was as tough as in any other school, and we slogged through the lessons unenthusiastically. By the time the third period began, almost everyone was sluggish. It was the maths period. Not our favourite subject.

'It's not fair. They expect us to study after all that drill and breakfast. Come on, guys, give us a break! I feel ready to hit the sack,' Maachh yawned.

'Rightly said, brother,' Bertie replied, and stretched his limbs. I glanced at his notebook, which was full of doodles.

Mr Kuldip Singh, our mathematics instructor, never carried any book. He was grey and had over thirty years of teaching experience at the Academy.

'Open page seventy-four of your book,' he instructed. 'I shall do sum numbers six, nine, and fifteen of exercise no. twelve, and thereafter, you guys can complete the exercise,' he announced, proceeding to solve the stated sums.

The point here is that the guy knew each page of the book and what was on it. That was the kind of memory I would have liked to attain.

'I'll take a nap while you copy the sums,' Maachh said, stretching his legs under the table.

Dutifully, I copied the sums, while Bertie continued to draw females with extra large mammaries, in his rough notebook.

The much-awaited siren finally announced the end of our classes.

'Boy, I could do with some nice lunch,' declared Randy pedalling furiously towards the mess.

'Do you guys ever think of anything but food?' I asked, irritated with their obsession with the subject.

'Of course, we do.' It was Bertie. 'We think of girls. Don't you?'

'Get serious,' I reprimanded. The science test announced in the class had dampened my sense of humour.

'Why the grouchy behaviour, buddy?' Bertie persisted.

'I know, it is the test that disturbs our studious pal,' Randy smirked.

We literally threw our bikes into the stand, dropped the satchels and books in the nearest cabin of our course mate, and scampered down for lunch to the mess, in squads.

I had heard of depressed people taking solace in food, but we were a suppressed lot resorting to food therapy. With satisfied sighs, we buried our snouts in the nosebags, and did full justice to the cook's creations. The dessert arrived, and we waited with our spoons in hand, ready to attack the delicious-looking pudding. We goaded Patrick to hasten his serving.

Just then arrived the pale-face, a fifth-term senior. He sauntered to our table and snarled, 'Halt! Numbskulls, you can't touch the dessert till you tell me its name.'

It was one of those exotic French puddings that had a mile-long string of unpronounceable syllables, enough to baffle the most brilliant minds. I stared at the dish thoughtfully, willing it to speak for itself. Across me, Natty's Adam's apple was dancing dangerously, as he exercised his grey cells. Seated by his side,

Maachh looked dolefully at the sunshine yellow and cream concoction and gulped. His salivary glands were activated already.

A victorious gleam in his eyes, the tormentor strutted towards Bertie's end. Taking the opportunity, like Aladdin's genie in waiter's garb, Patrick quietly slid to my side and muttered under his breath, 'Clafoutis aux abricots.'

I could barely pronounce the dish but made a valiant attempt at it, startling everyone around me. The senior stared wordlessly at me, his jaw half an inch below its normal location, while we attacked the dessert with gusto.

'You were great pal,' praised Bertie, on our way back to the squadron.

'What beats me is how you discovered the tongue-twisting, nose stuffing French name.'

'There should be some law against using foreign names in the dining hall,' protested Maachh. 'It is unpatriotic. I bet the French will not be able to pronounce rosogolla, to save their lives.' A loud burp cut off the rest of his opinion.

'I will settle for good old custard any day. It is simple, both for eating and pronouncing,' laughed Randy.

The rest of the run back to the squadron was silent. We wondered whether we would be allowed to grab some rest before the extra classes and games. That was not to be as we were sent packing on some errands by the sixth-termers.

The only person who seemed quite pleased with running errands was Bertie. He had been asked by a sixthy to buy some fags from the Gole Market. Although smoking was banned, the sixth-termers smoked freely in their rooms and corridors. When their stock of fags finished, they sent one of the first-termers to the Gole Market to replenish their supplies.

The Gole Market, the only shopping place within the Academy, was so named because of its round shape. Hardly a market, it had a couple of shops that catered to almost all the needs of the cadets. An errand to the Gole Market was always welcome, as this was the only place where one could loiter around for some time without any fear of ragging. Besides, it was the only place where one could spot a female.

That evening, all first-termers were shown a film on table manners. I guess someone must have observed our unfettered pigging style in the mess and thought it appropriate to educate us about the subject. We were, after all, expected to graduate as officers and gentlemen.

Later, I learnt that it was part of the training. Several instructive films on etiquette, customs, hygiene, sexually transmitted diseases, and similar subjects were a part of the curriculum.

Maachh's snoring all through the documentary was a terrible distraction. He was not the only one. The darkened auditorium resonated with snores, effectively altering the acoustics of the place.

'A great place to catch forty winks,' Harry announced, slumping down in his seat.

'Pessi,' commanded Bertie. 'Tell me what the film was all about on our way back to the squadron.'

I cursed the lot. No wonder they exhibited no manners at the dining table. I was also piqued by the moniker they had coined for me. It was Bertie's idea. Overnight, from decent Nick, I became Pessi, short for 'pessimist'.

Refreshed after the snooze, Maachh seemed to be in a good mood, while mine had worsened as we moved to the parade ground for games. It got darker by the minute as I kicked the football around. I felt more like a blind mouse than a rat. At least a rat knew where he was heading. Our hours had been crammed with so much activity that I hadn't had time to pause and take stock. Now it seemed as though I had been running from one task to the other without any respite, and the added tension of a test looming in the horizon cast a shadow on my mood. When would I study? What if

I couldn't get good grades? I could visualize my father sneering as he mouthed his favourite expression in front of Mom, 'I told you so. The army needs brains, and your son doesn't have any.'

'Hey numbskull, where is your attention?' yelled a sixthy, as the ball flew across my line of vision. 'Can't you see the ball coming, or don't you have the balls to play a straight game?'

I was thrown out of the field and told to run around the entire field, twice. I passed Maachh at another end of the field, playing hockey. He gave me a thumbs-down indication, and I wanted nothing better than to squeeze his giraffe-neck.

The mood didn't improve with dinner, either. It must have been infectious because I found both Bertie and Maachh looking sullen as we walked back from the mess.

'Bloody sadists,' cursed Bertie. 'Can't leave a guy alone.'

No one bothered to respond.

'I am not going back to the squadron.'

Everyone knew that returning to the squadron would mean another round of tasks from the seniors. It wasn't the errands that bothered us, but the fact that we could never please them. Each task invariably ended up with punishments, most of us landing up at the seventh heaven. In any case, it was Sunday night, and no one liked to run errands on a Sunday night.

'I feel like having a fag,' declared Randy.

'Are you crazy?' I hissed.

'Don't worry, Pessi, I won't get you in trouble,' he assured me confidently.

Just because I didn't display a reckless streak, I was a pessimist, according to them.

'And how do you intend smoking?' I countered.

'Don't strain the wee brain, pal.'

'Hey, that was a good line.' Bertie butted in. 'Rhyming strain and brain, a good touch, really. You are in the wrong profession, Randy; you could try your hand at becoming a poet.'

'I know just the place for a quiet fag,' said Randy, as he led us to a derelict battle tank with a missing hatch, placed right in front of the Sudan Block. He jumped inside the contraption with the aplomb of a victor.

'This was captured by our forces from the Pakis during the war,' he informed the three of us. 'Today, it shall have the honour of housing four first-term cadets who wish to smoke in secret,' he ended.

'Hear, hear,' cheered Bertie, struggling with the rusted nails of the broken seat.

We took a few puffs each from the cigarette Randy conjured up from his pocket. Even I relented by taking a couple of drags. The idea of smoking inside a captured battle tank had a special appeal, and soon we began to relax.

'This is a good hiding place, yaar,' Maachh chanted while trying to blow smoke rings. All he managed was a splutter and cough as the smoke rushed from his nostrils in an unmanageable wave.

It was a full moon night, and we felt like war heroes in the captured tank. Unexpectedly, our mood turned upbeat. Life began to look rosy. The future seemed promising as we looked beyond ragging. Through a haze of smoke, Bertie admired the Sudan block, contrasted magnificently against the ink-blue sky.

'What do you think would happen if one was to place a riding hat on top of the mast on Sudan Block?' he asked.

I threw him a horrified look.

'I didn't ask you, Pessi,' he rebuked me gently. Turning to the others, he asked, 'Say, what do you guys think of the idea?'

Maachh was seriously contemplating the steering rods of the tank jutting out near him.

'I wish I could drive this ruddy thing out on the Academy road,' he mused.

'Wouldn't it shock the chaps out of their wits?'

'You guys are lunatics. Raving madcaps,' I ranted.

'So, as I was saying,' continued Bertie, ignoring my outburst. 'What do you think would happen if I were to place my riding hat there?' he pointed at the top of the mast.

'You wouldn't dare,' challenged Randy.

'Oh yes, I would.'

'Challenge?' Both Maachh and Randy goaded him on.

My intervention had no effect on the chaps. They were discussing the quantum of the wager as I walked back to the squadron, leaving them to their fate.

On Monday morning, as we cycled towards the Sudan Block, we saw a group of cadets staring and pointing towards the top of the building. The crowd began swelling. Looking up to see the reason for the traffic jam, I noticed the damn thing. There it was – a riding hat poised proudly on the flag mast. I threw a shocked look at Rebello who was coolly cruising along. His nonchalance made me burst into laughter.

'You bloody fool,' I addressed the hero. 'You did it!'

'A challenge is a challenge, and the Rebellos are not known to shy away from accepting one,' he remarked, his face creased in a sublime smile.

The guy had stirred up not one but a series of hornet nests. Like angry wasps the sixth-term office holders and ustaads buzzed around in their efforts to pin down the culprit. When the manhunt failed to yield results, the entire lot of cadets paid for the mischief by going up to the glider-drome and back, wearing their bicycles around the neck, a distance of almost seven kilometres. For most cadets, it was worth it.

For the three of us, Bertie was a hero. Maachh and Randy lost a hundred rupees each, payable in installments since none of them possessed that amount. Rebello's chest swelled to double its size, and he strutted around importantly for the rest of the week.

Every evening, the first-termers turned into an entertaining troupe in the anteroom. We were supposed to enter the anteroom before the others, and entertain the second-termers with dance, songs or mimicry, till the sixth-termers arrived. Bertie was much in demand during the entertainment hour as he was one of the few who could sing a decent note, while the others competed with the donkeys from the dhobi ghat.

A week into the first term was the intro-night. I was quite anxious about the event, as I had heard some very disquieting rumours.

'It is nothing, yaar, just an intro as the name suggests,' Maachh tried to dispel my apprehension.

'But we have to introduce ourselves wearing nothing more than our undies.'

'Where is the problem? After you have bathed in the nude with the guys, undies are a fair degree of dressing up.'

I was still quite nervous. It is one thing to undress in a bathroom, and quite another to stand in underwear before an audience, and introduce oneself. Add to that my stage fright and you have a perfect case of intro-phobia.

Maachh had a fantastic idea. 'Let's anoint our bodies with a lot of hair oil,' he suggested.

'Are you crazy?' I objected. 'We will smell like Banke Bihari from Jhumri Tallayya.'

'Pessi, are you as stupid as you appear, or is it a put-on?' he scolded.

'The oil will make us slippery enough to elude the grabbing hands.'

'Don't tell me!' I was horrified. This piece of news was disquieting. 'Are they going to grab us?'

'Yes, my dear innocent babe. They will maul you if you don't manage to slip out fast enough.'

The five of us poured a couple of bottles of highly scented hair oil that Bertie had pilfered from some first-termer's room.

It was a highly strung self that entered the squadron anteroom on the intro-night. The lights had been suitably dimmed for the occasion, in deference to our state of undress, but the music was loud. I found it an infantile psychological attempt at lulling the nerves. I had already reached the end of my tether.

'All you have to do is stand in front of the squadron, introduce yourself, and then bolt across the anteroom and out,' my mates reassured me.

Despite their attempts at nonchalance, I could detect the jumpiness in their voices.

It isn't easy to face a jeering lot of seniors bent upon making your life hell, clad in nothing but your basic fig leaf.

Ranade was the first one to go before the crowd of seniors. As he introduced himself in a tremulous octave, the audience went berserk. They hooted and whistled, and he turned a pasty yellow, his face the hue of a poached egg. I half expected him to collapse, but he managed to blurt out his lines and scamper across the hall.

There was a melee as hands reached out to grab his underwear, and he struggled to protect his dignity. Next, it was Harry, the surd. He seemed totally unaffected by all the hooting and booing as he closed his eyes and made his speech. Thereafter, he bolted like an Olympics sprinter, but his speed couldn't save him from losing his underwear at the hands of a few fourth-termers blocking the exit.

It was Rebello's turn now. He went up and began singing 'Silent night, holy night', effectively creating a trance. There was absolute silence as the cadets tried to come to terms with his act. Before they could react to his con act, he made a quick getaway.

Smart guy! I wished I had the presence of mind to think up something as stunning.

One by one, all the first-termers introduced themselves in their unique characteristic manner. Hands pounced on the chaps, and stripped them if they were slow to make an exit. The smooth-skinned and cute-looking guys had a tough time as they were delayed for long and subjected to a lot of discomfort before being let off.

Finally, it was my turn. I strode up with trembling innards. I had practised the short speech at least a dozen times in the room, but the cat got my tongue the minute I stood before the crowd.

I froze. I just couldn't speak. The crowd hollered and hooted, but my tongue seemed to have got glued to my palate. And then Bertie came to my rescue. From one dark corner of the room he began singing 'Jingle bells, jingle bells, jingle all the way.' That was my cue.

A hush fell over the gathering as they wondered if it was some kind of a planned programme. I quickly uttered the perfunctory sentences and made my getaway while the attention was diverted, narrowly missing the hands that reached out for me.

As soon as the song ended, the seniors began shouting.

'Where are the buffoons? The *** buffoons?'

They were hunting for both Bertie and me, but we had lost ourselves in the darkness of the hall.

In celebration of Bertie's heroic rescue stunt, we decided to go for the movie show that Sunday evening. The Academy movie theatre was a popular haunt for the cadets. It was a massive structure with two balconies at different levels. The lower balcony was meant for the instructors and their families, and the upper one for junior cadets. Twice a week, on Saturdays and Sundays, the theatre screened movies, which provided a suitable diversion for the hard-working cadets.

The rules were strict. Hooting or whistling was not allowed, not even when the vamp gyrated sexily to a hot number. In case a cadet let out a whistle under the cover of darkness, assuming that it would go undetected, the entire lot had to pay for the mischief. The mass punishment meted out for the misdemeanour was a tough one. We had to roll all the way to the mess, which was quite a distance away.

Come Sunday and we dressed carefully in our muftis. It was the first time for us. We felt like prisoners on parole.

'Wow! Think of all the girls who would be there,' Bertie's eyes were enlarged to saucer size as he performed an impromptu depiction of a female form with his hands. 'Man, I just can't wait to be there.'

'Watch your step, Bertie,' I warned. 'You can get electrocuted if you touch the wrong wires.'

'Oh, Pessi, keep your warnings to yourself,' he replied carelessly. 'Do you think I am going to miss the only chance of meeting a female in the Academy by playing Cautious Carl, my pal?'

I shrugged resignedly. Bertie never looked before leaping. I couldn't teach him to do so now. I just reminded him that about a thousand cadets had the same idea while going for a movie.

A host of senior office holders were seen hovering around the theatre, indulging in a popular sport – eyeing the instructors' daughters. We were in for a surprise when we reached the theatre. All the first-termers were promptly herded into the top balcony. Bertie rushed towards the front row hoping to steal a look at the imaginary girls gathered below.

'Hey man, the hall is deserted!' he squealed, his voice thick with disappointment.

A voice rang out from the back.

'So, what did you expect? We guys are supposed to enter the hall half an hour before the show, and leave only half an hour after the show finishes, when all the others have gone home. Stop daydreaming and settle down.'

After much craning of the neck, a game in which Maachh had an advantage, given his giraffe-neck, we got a royal crick and all we saw was more cadets trooping into the ground floor area. Not a single female was visible.

Bertie's idea of taking a leak during the interval yielded no benefit either, as the toilets for the cadets were also on the same floor. We were totally isolated from the others.

By now, all of us had lost interest in the movie. Maachh was already snoring, his head propped on my shoulder.

'Shucks, man!' Randy swore. 'What is the point of taking all the trouble? Might as well loll around the Gole Market or catch up on sleep.'

Much after the movie was over, we were led out in small groups. It was totally dark outside. We saw the whole lot of cadets front-rolling back to the mess. Without any questions, we joined in. 'What a let-down,' cursed Maachh, refreshed after his snooze. 'All this rolling for nothing!'

The mess was a long distance from the theatre. If one were to roll honestly, the spine was sure to get all bent and twisted, so we cheated. We slid towards the darkest parts of the road where there were no street lights. Some cadets crept and crawled, rolling occasionally. Some managed to dash into the bushes by the roadside, under the cover of darkness, and hid there till everyone had rolled by.

The roll back to the mess was not entirely devoid of fun. Cadets always managed to introduce an element of excitement in the toughest of ordeals. Life couldn't go on otherwise, given the misfortunes that haunted the first-termers. It was simply a matter of creative thinking.

Randy charged into a fifth-term sergeant who was standing in a secluded spot, and knocked him down by ramming his head into the senior's belly. The sergeant fell flat on his back, and Randy vanished. The sergeant got up and gave a chase, but it was impossible to catch Randy who sprinted as though his life depended upon it. Frustrated, the sergeant came back and kicked everyone on their backside, commanding them to roll faster. All the first to fifth-termers rolled together with great solidarity. When asked if anyone knew the name of the offender, no one responded. He kicked us some more till his foot got weary. We would have done our nation proud in the event of being captured by the enemy.

Randy was our hero for the evening. He had done what everyone wanted to do.

'I wish I had hit the bugger,' lamented Bertie.

'So do I,' seconded Maachh.

At the squadron, it became a challenge for all first-termers to repeat Randy's feat. At the next movie just after the show, when we were ordered to roll back to the mess, Ravi Sukhdev charged like a bull with his head down and rammed into a sergeant, knocking him down. The next instant, he vanished into the cover of darkness. The sergeant ran after him, but Ravi was too swift for him. We weren't surprised when he later went on to hold the 400-m low hurdles record at the NDA.

From that day, it became a challenge for the first-termers to hit and dodge. Those who could evade being caught were heroes, and those who couldn't, were reduced to a zero.

FIVE

There was a shortcut from our squadron to the Sudan Block that would have saved us a good 500 metres on our way to classes, but we were banned from using it since it would mean coming over from the wrong side.

'Darn these rules,' cribbed Maachh. 'Here we are, always running short of time, and we can't use a route that would save us a good two minutes.'

'I am going to do it, guys,' announced Bertie.

We stared at him as though he had gone bonkers. Daring to use the wrong side of the path in broad daylight was suicidal. No one in his right frame of mind would do it. But then Bertie was a madcap. He just had to do the forbidden things, and no one could convince him otherwise.

'It would mean another string of punishments for the entire lot,' I tried to dissuade him.

'It will be worth the punishment,' he said. He had the last word, as usual.

He was not the only one; there were some crazy cadets who

would sneak through the short cut whenever no ustaad was lurking around. For Bertie, it was a challenge.

Sure enough, the next afternoon he took the short cut while going back to the squadron after classes. He was spotted in the act by an alert ustaad, who immediately gave a chase.

'Halt, cadet!' he hollered, but Bertie wasn't heeding. He led the ustaad a merry chase, and just as the ustaad was finally catching up with him, Rebello entered the squadron, went up to the first floor, and jumped to the ground. Before he could pick himself up and run, the ustaad also jumped from the first floor and landed on him.

The ustaad dusted himself, stood up and roared: 'Nonsense, cadet! Short cut leta hai!(Nonsense, cadet! You took a short cut!)'.

Bertie was immediately booked. The charge read, 'Taking a short cut from first floor to the ground floor.'

There couldn't have been five guys more different than us. Maachh, with his typical Bong accent and predilection for fish and mischief, thought up the weirdest of plans. Quite a physical guy with no interest in the finer arts, he was at his comical best when trying to attract girls' attention at the Gole Market. Bertie called him the 'Tragedy King' because he was the first one to get caught when things went wrong. His days were chequered with punishments.

In contrast to Maachh, Bertie was the musical kind. He could play the guitar as well as a mouth organ quite proficiently, but it was his rich voice that drew people to him. When he sang, you were forced to stop and listen. But he was also a good athlete. I had never seen anyone do a headstand without support the way Bertie could – he must have had a very strong neck. Another factor that set him apart from Maachh was the fact that he could put others in trouble and escape unscathed. He was the biggest prankster in the G squadron, yet he got away most of the time.

Randy was always precise, in most things. He conducted himself like an officer, walked straight, and was the best dressed guy around. These qualities did not, however, deter him from playing practical jokes on others. His impressive personality made him a natural leader.

As for Natty, the chap was content playing second fiddle to everyone. He loved movies, and every Sunday, he could be seen at the theatre, notwithstanding the rolling afterward.

As compared to them, I was just an ordinary person who wanted to finish the Academy training with good grades and make my father proud. Never a catalyst for trouble, I got caught up in the mischief because of the company I kept. I was the bridle that tried to restrain the wild horses, quite unsuccessfully. But I never gave up trying.

We became close not by choice, but due to the fact that our cabins were on the same side of the central lobby. We begged, borrowed, and did everything together.

The next day, we found Maachh front-rolling in the morning; on the seventh heaven in the afternoon; and doing Puttie Parades in the evening. Poor Maachh, he had never suffered so much.

When I asked him the cause of all the punishment, he let forth a volley of abuses.

'That ***SCC! One of these days, I am going to wipe the smirk off his face forever,' he ranted.

'But what did you do to upset him so much?'

'Arrey! All I did was break his favourite cup, and he got as mad as a bear with bees in his mouth. One would think he was the Mughal emperor, Jahangir, who had punished a slave with severe lashings because his favourite wine cup had been broken.'

Maachh liked to exaggerate. That was his major fault. 'I am going to teach him a lesson.'

He seemed determined to do something rash. My efforts at pacifying the obstinate Bong, met with no success.

'Let it pass. No point making more trouble.' I said, putting on the big-brother act.

The next morning, we found him grinning from ear to ear as he carried the SCC's tea. 'Hang around. I want you guys to witness a great moment in history,' Maachh instructed us.

Even as I wondered what was wrong with the tea, we found Maachh rolling helplessly with laughter after handing over the mug to the SCC.

'That's my piss he is drinking,' he informed us cheerfully. We stared at him as though he had suddenly transformed into a multi-headed serpent from a mythological movie.

'Commendable,' muttered Randy. 'Quite commendable! I hadn't thought you capable of such creative thinking.'

Maachh had extracted his revenge by urinating in the SCC's mug of tea.

Obviously, the change in flavour didn't have much impact on the senior because he continued to make Maachh fetch his tea.

There was something about Maachh that invited trouble. He had a foot constantly poised on problems, and landed on his face most of the time.

We had to go past the NTT (Naval Training Team) office on our way to the morning classes. One day, on the way back, Macchh's bike had a flat. We left him to deal with the problem and rushed back. It made me sorry that I could not stop and help a guy in trouble, but then, it was just not possible to do so without getting into difficulty myself.

As the poor chap was returning on the double with his bike, a naval officer stopped him in front of the NTT office and screamed, 'You, first-termer, why didn't you salute?'

'I didn't see you, sir,' Maachh replied bravely.

'I am standing right in your path and you say that you didn't see me. Are you blind?' the officer barked. 'Who is your squadron commander? Report to him immediately.'

Poor Maachh! He knew he was sunk. The chap was sure to complain. Panting, he returned to the squadron, parked his bike, and reported to the squadron commander, Squadron Leader Jain.

'You clumsy baboon, are you blind?' demanded Jain. Obviously, the naval officer had made his call.

'Sir, I didn't notice him,' Maachh continued to defend himself with the same excuse.

'Not good enough. Try a more convincing reply, or I'll send you for a high jump (the Sinhgad hike),' threatened Jain.

'Sir, actually, he didn't look like an officer,' Maachh finally came out with the truth.

'Get lost, you louse!' Jain shouted, trying to suppress his smile. 'Next time I get a complaint from the NTT, you'll curse the day you were born.'

Macchh could not believe his luck. He had been let off without punishment. He sprinted back to us, looking like a penguin that had just had a ride on a glacier. His story soon spread around the squadron and he became an instant hero.

The mother of all pains was the cross-country practice, which we tried to avoid like the flu. For the guys who were not good at any game like hockey, football or basketball, it was a nightmare since they were made to practise cross-country all the time.

For whatever reason, the instructors seemed to lay a lot of importance on the damned event. Maybe it was their fear that during the war, we would not be able to run fast enough over the hurdles if we didn't practise hard enough. Anyway, cross-country competition was accorded prime importance, and it was mandatory for every cadet to participate in it. Cadets who didn't fare well in it didn't stand a chance of making it to the next term.

So we ran the eight-kilometre distance, climbing over a lone tree hill, scrambling over mounds, tumbling down the slopes, in the shortest possible time. The target was to reduce the timing by all possible means, because those who could not make it in good time were made to run every day.

Golf squadron's record for the cross-country competition was dismal. Of the twelve positions, the squadron had never managed to rise above the tenth place.

It was a shame because cross-country competition carried the maximum weight while the overall championship was considered. Since the squadron officers were graded according to the performance of their squadrons, they fretted over our performance. We were promised the moon if we did well, and hell if we did not.

Desperate to pull us out of the rut of double digits, our officers sweated along with us. The cadets were put through rigorous practice, which started a month in advance. All this so that we could break the jinx. Needless to say, it was the first-termers who were expected to bring in the laurels since the sixth-termers were an elite lot. Each Sunday morning, the officers of the squadron would turn up to check the progress of their squadron. Cadets who did well could go on liberty to Poona and were allowed more freedom. Those who did not fare well were made to suffer punishments like running daily during the games period, and curtailing of privileges. Liberty, as the very name suggests, was our passport to a visit to the city on Sundays. For the cadets who had slogged through the week, it was a big event. To be denied liberty was the most heartbreaking punishment that could be given to a cadet.

As luck would have it, during the practice runs, the officers concentrated on the first-termers and allowed the seniors to practise on their own. The scoundrels invariably took short cuts, while we ran in real earnest. In fact, the onus of our failure rested entirely on the sixth-termers who cheated during the practice runs.

It was a glorious Sunday morning and after a hectic night of punishments, we were in no mood for the cross-country practice run. Sullen-faced, we made our way to the field.

'It is sinful to run on a beautiful morning like this,' remarked Bertie. 'A morning like this is meant for picnics. I could think of ...'

'Why don't you invite Sabby for a picnic?' interjected Maachh. 'I am sure he won't mind cooking your goose.'

Sabby was Captain Sabharwal, our squadron officer.

'Shut up,' said Bertie angrily, his temper on the boil.

'Move it, guys, move it,' Randy goaded. 'Don't squander your energy over silly matters. When the rape is inevitable, it is better to lie down and enjoy it.' We prepared ourselves for the rape of our morning.

The general practice followed by the officers was to flag off the run at 6.00 a.m., after which they stayed back at the starting point, armed with stop watches to time the cadets.

Eager to finish the ordeal, the cadets took off as fast as they could. As soon as we were beyond the visibility range of the officers, Maachh halted. He signalled us to slow down and allow the other cadets to overtake us. He said, 'I don't want to run all the distance. I hate cross-country runs.'

'So what's new? We all hate it,' said Bertie.

'The seniors always take a short cut, while we are made to sweat. Let us skip the lone tree hill,' suggested Maachh.

'And?' I asked.

'We will take a short cut,' he said, and watched us for our reactions.

Randy didn't offer any response, so I also restrained myself. Maachh continued to outline his plan. 'Here's what we will do. We will rest under the cover of the bushes near the hillock. When we see the first lot of the cadets returning from the lone tree hill, we will emerge from our hideout and join them. That way, we will be among the first lot, without having to run all the way.'

He waited eagerly for the applause he expected for his brilliant plan. There was none.

'But that is cheating,' I was indignant.

'No one is stopping you, Pessi. Why don't you run till the farthest point, my dear Gandhi?' Bertie spoke up.

That shut me up. Gandhi was the moniker I hated more than Pessi. From decent Nick, I had tumbled to becoming Pessi, and now they were deifying me into the Father of the Nation.

With all of them agreeing to Maachh's dim-witted plan, I hardly had any option.

'Let's creep towards the bushes on the return route,' suggested Randy. 'But for heaven's sake, be cautious. The last thing we want is to get caught in the act.'

'Wait till the others have passed by,' I cautioned nervously.

It could be disastrous if someone spotted us. The entire lot of hillocks was crawling with cadets.

The moment everyone had crossed us, we began creeping under the cover of bushes, towards the return route. The hillocks offered us adequate cover.

We had almost made it to the clump of bushes near the finishing point.

'One last dash, and we will be there,' I sighed with relief as we crouched and sped to the undergrowth. Suddenly, we froze in our tracks. Someone was already there behind the bushes. Perplexed, we shushed at each other and crept stealthily towards the culprit. It had to be another smart cadet like us.

And the next instant Captain Sabharwal sprang out of the bushes and seized Maachh, who was the first in line.

'You piddly little first-termers!' he yelled. 'You think you are smart, don't you? I knew some of you would try this stunt. Taking a short cut while the others are sweating it out? No wonder you smell as fresh as lilies. Wait till I make you sweat!'

And make us sweat he did.

He made us do the entire stretch again. We were back in the evening doing it yet again. Added to this, we were awarded three Sinhgad hikes, each.

I cursed Maachh for his dumb ideas.

'You really think you are smart,' I said, losing my cool. 'Sabby must have experienced dozens of cadets trying to outwit him. He knows all the tricks.'

The morning had been ruined beyond redemption. For once the Tragedy King had the wisdom to hold his tongue.

The punishment of hiking up to the Sinhgad fort was known as 'high jump', and it was not confined to first-termers only. Cadets from all terms and squadrons ran together.

The Sinhgad hike was reserved for Sundays. Sinhgad Fort had been a bastion of Shivaji, the valiant Maratha king who had the audacity to challenge the Mughal rulers. Perched on a steep hill, it was about twenty kilometres away from the Academy. The hike involved a climb of 800 metres on foot. More than the distance and altitude, it was the impossible deadline allotted to complete the hike that made the punishment rigorous. The cadets started off at 5.00 in the morning, and had to return by 3.00 p.m. The fort was a popular picnic spot for city folk, and every Sunday, luxury buses would disgorge hordes of them. For the cadets, however, it was no picnic as they hiked up, racing against time.

An officer or ustaad was posted near the entrance of the fort to mark the attendance of the cadets who reported there. Using unfair means like taking a lift from a passing vehicle, or cycling up (not that it was possible), was forbidden to the cadets.

The next Sunday, while the others were still in bed, we woke up early, changed into our battle order dress, and assembled at the PT ground for our first Sinhgad hike.

We were bursting with excitement.

'It will be fun going up,' said Randy. 'The place is full of girls who come for picnics.'

Bertie rubbed his hands gleefully at the prospect.

Maachh was equally enthusiastic about the idea.

'Let us hope we are able to complete the hike within the allotted time,' I began. 'Otherwise ...'

'Forever the dampener,' Randy cut me off. 'Pessi, your glass is forever half empty. You must learn to enjoy life.'

Darkness covered the Academy as we began our hike. A lot of ground had to be covered, and so, we started off at a fast clip. That morning, there were about fifteen of us. Among the star-crossed fifteen were some veterans who had been to Sinhgad a couple of times earlier.

'Let's get it over, fast,' I said, eager to get moving. 'If we are not able to complete the hike in time, the trip will not be counted.'

'What's the hurry? The entire day is at our disposal,' said Randy. 'Bertie, can't you get the chit for me from the ustaad on top?'

'My foot! You get one for me – you are faster with your legs,' said Bertie. He was one up on him.

By the time we began running, the others had already disappeared beyond the bend. My gang seemed to be in a mood to go slow. They ambled along at a leisurely pace amidst much bantering and backslapping as though they were off on a picnic. Maachh was at his irritating best, humming like a bumblebee, tunelessly. My efforts to convince them that this was no pleasure trip failed to galvanize them into a faster trot.

The lush green surroundings and the cool breeze were invigorating. We skirted the Khadakvasala Lake, and moved out of the NDA campus.

'Isn't it a spectacular view? Makes me want to pitch a tent and live here forever,' sighed Bertie.

'Keep your sacred dreams for a later date. Right now all you need to do is hasten your trot, dear comrade,' I admonished.

'Yes, it is better to run fast and reach the fort, and then loiter around. Then we can eye the girls in peace,' Maachh panted out, seconding my opinion.

By the time we reached the foothills, none of the other cadets were in sight. Wisdom dawned, and at last my pals realized that we were much behind schedule. That spurred their feet, and we began to run in earnest. In the next two hours, we covered a lot of ground. At the base of the hill, a few tourist buses and private vehicles had already arrived.

We covered almost fifteen kilometres wordlessly, and reached the toughest part. From here on, the climb was almost vertical.

'Let's take a break,' panted Bertie. 'I could do with a soft drink.'

'Forget the soft drink. Let's move,' I urged.

A few tea stalls had begun rolling up their shutters, and the aroma of steaming tea tickled our noses irresistibly. Despite all my motivating words, the team decided to take a tea break. We rested for a while savouring the brew served in chipped glasses, while our eyes darted energetically, feasting our tired eyes on a bevy of young girls standing near a tourist bus. It was with great reluctance that we relinquished the glasses and took to the road once again.

The picnickers looked at us with curiosity, watching us panting and puffing. Our shirts were already sticking to our backs, with the sweat running down in torrents. Taking pity on us, a few tourists offered us cold drinks, but common sense prevailed, and my pals turned down the offer. Each minute mattered, each moment vital.

Suddenly, Randy screeched to an abrupt halt. Looking back I realized that it would be difficult to drag him away from the spot. Some of the girls smiled and waved at Randy, who smiled back at them. With his tall, athletic figure and handsome features, he always managed to attract female attention. Bertie also lingered back hopefully.

'Come on, you two,' I pleaded.

'You guys, carry on. I will join you in a few minutes,' Randy said, ignoring my plea, and fell behind, while Bertie hesitated. After a few moments, he decided to continue the run.

'No point in encouraging them,' he said gravely.

'Grapes are sour,' sang Maachh in a nasal undertone.

'No one even stops to look at guys like us,' Maachh cribbed a while later, once we were running again.

'Don't worry, buddy,' I consoled, 'once we pass out of the Academy, there will be hordes of girls lining up, and you won't know whom to choose.'

That set his mind at rest. 'Do you think so?' he asked hopefully.

En route we found several cadets lolling around the parking area where a group of girls had gathered. They pretended to drink water, but it was obvious that they had taken a break for some bird watching. Although Bertie and Maachh were tempted to linger on, sanity prevailed, and they continued with the hike.

Gradually, the three of us gained ground and were soon leading the pack. The shortest route to the fort was through a steep, almost vertical climb. Most cadets preferred the easier, circuitous route, which naturally took more time. Mercifully, my friends agreed to the suggestion that we take the shorter route.

The fort was impressive. With its rugged features, the impenetrable bastion evoked visions of yesteryear. The steep sides, which made the fort invincible for the Marathas, made it equally tough for us to scale. It seemed hours before, totally spent, we panted up to the top. I plonked myself on a boulder and pointed at the army jeep parked at the entrance of the fort. The ustaad seated inside glanced at us and put down his newspaper. We were the first cadets to have reached the top.

'Good, very good, cadet, shaabash (well done)!' He thumped our backs energetically and proceeded to complete the formality of marking our attendance in the register, after which he handed us the chits, which were a proof that we had reported at the top.

Waving the piece of paper philosophically, Maachh said, 'Isn't it funny? This bit of paper represents hours of energy and perspiration.'

'Keep it safe, buddy. It is the only proof that we trudged all the way here,' cautioned Bertie.

Like spent bubbles in a flat drink, we lay limply on the grass and stared at the blue, cloudless sky. The sun had turned into a ball of fury, singeing everything in sight, but we didn't have the energy to get up and move into shade. Pulling our caps low over our eyes, we continued to bask there. The thrill of visiting Sinhgad had already fizzled out. We were sweating through all possible pores in our body.

After a while, the skin almost blistering with heat, we decided to embark on our return journey.

'Shall we wait for Randy?' I asked Maachh.

'Not necessary.' The green monster of jealousy seemed to have coiled around his heart. 'He will find his way when he finishes with the girls.'

'But we came together,' I protested. 'I think we should wait for him.'

'So do I,' added Bertie.

'Okay. Just five minutes, and then we return,' Maachh conceded.

The minutes ticked by, but there was no trace of Randy. Reluctantly, I got up. Not completing the hike in the stipulated time would amount to the trip being nullified.

As we were coming down, Maachh spied Randy taking the long, circuitous route with a group of girls in tow. Like a guide, he pointed to something in the horizon and the girls tittered. He seemed to be enjoying himself.

'He deserves a kick on his backside,' Maachh hissed through his teeth.

'Let him enjoy himself,' I responded, defending Randy.

'That guy is overconfident. Just because he is good at cross-country, he thinks he can make it in time to the top.'

He never did. Coming down last, Randy invited the ustaad's

wrath, and earned an extra visit to the fort.

'Have fun. I am sure you will enjoy the extra hike,' Maachh said sarcastically when Randy informed us about his punishment. We didn't envy him the extra trip; our experience of conquering Singhad had been anything but pleasurable.

After our first hike, we became smarter.

'We have to find a way to cut the trip short. There's got to be a simpler way to do it,' said Maachh, his brain cells working furiously.

I agreed. It wasn't worth spending that kind of time and energy.

Maachh and Bertie put their brains together and devised an innovative method of cheating.

'Here's what we do,' said Maachh. After much deliberation, they had come up with a feasible plan. 'On our next hike, we will take our bikes.'

'Forget it,' I decided to prick his balloon. 'If we are caught riding the bikes, we will have to do the hike every day.'

'You are an idiot, Pessi.' He scorned my concerns. 'At 5.00 in the morning, who do you think will be watching us in the darkness?'

'Okay, and where will we keep the bikes?' I persisted.

At this stage, Bertie took over from Maachh. 'We will ride under the cover of darkness up to the lake at the foothills, and leave them there.'

'Leave them in the open, near the lake?' I was incredulous.

Bertie threw me a pitying look. 'Sometimes, just sometimes, I have this strong urge to club you on your head.' Bertie's voice was hard. 'We will submerge them at an isolated spot of the lake. After that, we shall continue the trek to the top of the hill. It will save us a good hour or so. On the way back, all we have to do is retrieve the bikes and pedal back to the Academy.'

Their plan took the wind out of my sails. It was stupid but

workable. We tried it out several times with fantastic results. Soon, many cadets were sharing the subterfuge, and the edge of the lake was packed with submerged bicycles.

SIX

The ragging was too much to bear. A sense of depression gripped us the moment we were alone in our rooms. The days passed in a whirl of activities, but the nights seemed to haunt us. Despite all the tiredness, there were nights when I couldn't sleep. Homesickness gripped me like an anaconda, asphyxiating me and draining my life juices surely and slowly.

Written on the right-hand top corner of our classroom blackboard were a few enigmatic alphabets: DLTGH. To an outsider, they would mean nothing, but to the homesick cadets, they meant liberation from difficult days. The letters were an acronym for Days Left to Go Home. Our excitement rose in direct proportion to the reduction of DLTGH.

One night, as we escaped into our favourite T-55 tank in front of the Sudan Block for our fags, I was in a state of dark depression. The day had been unusually tough, packed as it had been with classes and punishments. Maachh was still under the grip of the CSM, and we wondered about his fate. Just then, Maachh burst into the battle tank. Gnashing his teeth, he declared that he wanted to murder the CSM. The poor chap's fingers were swollen and bruised. He had been hanging on the seventh heaven for a minor offence, and the effect was quite visible.

'One of these days I am going to remove all the wires from my ventilator,' he hissed.

We sympathized with his tormented soul, and assured him of our assistance in the matter of wire removal from all ventilators.

The derelict battle tank, with its missing hatch was our hideout, our own private domain, and we escaped there to enjoy a few puffs whenever the opportunity arrived.

The night was beautiful, but we were in a dejected mood. Drawing on our fags, we bared our souls to each other.

'I wish I could run away,' I confided. 'The ragging and the killing routine are getting too much for me.'

'Why don't you?' asked Bertie. 'I can't run away because I opted for this life. If I were to go back to Goa, my father would promptly put me into a college, force me to graduate in commerce, and then enroll my services for the family business. And one thing I am confident about is that this life is much better than sitting in the shop.'

'You have studied in a boarding school, so you don't miss your family, but I do.'

'That is why I am saying, run away. Go back to your family.'

'That's the problem. I can't,' I said, staring helplessly at the stars winking above me. 'I defied my father to join the NDA. If I go back, he will rub it in for the rest of my life.'

'Why did you want to join the Academy in the first place?' asked Randy.

'When we lived in Poona, I had several friends whose fathers were instructors at the Academy. They lived inside the campus, and I came here frequently to play with them. I attended a few Passing Out Parades, and that was it,' I confessed. 'I was hooked by the glamour and gleam.'

'What about you?' Bertie asked Maachh. 'Wouldn't you like to escape from here?'

'Me?' he looked incredulous. 'Banish the thought, my boy. My father has lived for the day I become an army officer. It is a follow-up of his boyhood dream. That is the reason he put me in a Sainik School right from the beginning. He will skin me alive if I were to run away from the Academy.'

Randy was the only one who seemed quite content with life, as he let out a cloud of smoke from his mouth.

'I'm okay,' he replied to Maachh's questioning look. 'I have never known any other life. Right from my great-grandfather to my brother, everyone has been in the army. It is a family tradition. I don't really mind the rigour. It sort of toughens you up, and then there are compensations. It isn't going to be like this forever. Imagine, a few terms later, we will be seniors. This too shall pass,' Randy ended philosophically.

All through our conversation, Natty had held his tongue. Now he spoke up, 'I've been tempted too. I have wanted to run away many times, but I can't.'

'And why is that, my dear chap?' asked Bertie.

'My school had given me a grand send-off when I left for the NDA. It would be a disgrace if I ran away from it. Imagine the kind of ridicule my entire family would have to face. Besides, I don't think my father can afford to pay the compensation that is required to be paid if I ditch the Academy.'

'Enough of this nonsense. Let's change the topic. I don't like depressive talk,' interjected Bertie. 'Why waste time over what can't be?'

But no one seemed to be in a mood to talk. A cloud had covered the sky, concealing the moon. The night no longer seemed to hold any enchantment for us. Lost in thought, we walked back to the squadron.

The gloom didn't desert me even upon reaching the room, so

I decided to borrow a book from Bertie. I found him seated at his desk, reading through a file labelled 'Gandhi's Teachings'. I was surprised. My take on the guy immediately went through mutation. A guy reading the lofty ideals of the Mahatma couldn't be a lost case, I thought. He must be deeper than he professed to be.

Even in my most abstemious state of mind, I had not resorted to reading writings by the Father of the Nation. Perhaps some sublime reading could lift me out of the blue.

He broke into loud guffaws when I asked if I could borrow the file.

'By all means,' he spluttered as he handed it to me.

I maintained a hurt and meaningful silence at his scorn as I left his room.

Switching on the table lamp, I prepared myself for some enlightenment. Maybe Gandhi's wisdom about the bare truths of life would guide me in my darkest hours. With a flourish, I opened the file and stared aghast. Stuck inside were pages and pages of voluptuous nudes torn out from *Playboy* and *Debonair*.

Later, I learnt that every cadet possessed his own collection of Gandhi's Teachings. Since putting up posters on the doors and walls was not allowed, the cadets did the next best thing – they made their personal scrapbooks adorned with female nudes. The next morning, I was the butt of all jokes. Maachh continued to call me Gandhiji for the next few weeks.

One evening, in the anteroom, Randy decided to play his harmonica. The guy was a natural. Like he did most things, he was pretty good at wielding the mouth organ, too. After he finished playing a foot-tapping song, a burst of applause rang through the hall, and a few first-termers crowded around him. So enchanted were they with his skill that they wanted him to tutor them on the instrument. Some senior cadets also joined the 'wannabe' pack of musicians. He agreed to teach the entire lot on the condition that each one got his own mouth organ.

Within a week, a dozen cadets had acquired mint condition mouth organs with 'Hero: Made in China' inscribed on them. From that day, the G squadron resonated with a cacophony of discordant notes at all odd hours of the day and night, except when the seniors were around. Many gave up after a day or two of valiant struggle, while a few had the patience to continue for a couple of weeks. By the end of the month, only a couple of patient ones were seen with their mouth organs. Grudgingly, I must admit that they could make reasonably refined noises.

One morning, Maachh sprang a surprise on us.

'I want you to meet a general,' he said.

Excited at the prospect, we flooded him with questions.

'Is he still in service?'

'Has he fought a war?'

'Is he an ex-NDA cadet?'

'Wait till you meet him,' was the enigmatic reply, as he led us towards the library.

Once we reached there, he sought out a senior cadet, and pointed him out to us.

'What kind of joke is this?' hissed Bertie. 'That is a cadet and not a general.'

'Stupid, he is General Seth,' insisted Maachh. 'You'd better salute him.'

We rushed out of the library and broke into loud laughter, while he grew increasingly angry.

'Ask anyone, and they will confirm whatever I have told you.'

He caught hold of a friendly second-termer emerging from the library, for confirmation.

'He is right,' the guy seconded Maachh. 'That is General Seth.'

'But he is just a cadet.'

'Didn't you guys know that there are several brigadiers and generals in the Academy?' The second termer explained, 'A cadet who gets relegated once is called a brigadier, one who is relegated twice is a general, and a third-timer is called field marshal.'

Much to Maachh's chagrin, we just couldn't stop laughing at the information.

Each course, we discovered, had a couple of brigadiers and two or three generals, although field marshals were rare.

'I wouldn't mind becoming a general in the Academy,' said Bertie.

Among the cadets, there was a grudging respect for the generals.

'Nor would I,' seconded Maachh.

'Go hang yourselves,' I admonished. 'Do you know what you'll have to do to achieve that title?'

'We have to fail in our academics, or outdoor activities.'

'There is an easier way. I have found out. All you have to do is to get admitted into the hospital and lose a couple of weeks' training,' said Randy.

'With Mademoiselle Cruella ruling the MI Room, do you think that is possible?' laughed Bertie. 'She will hang us upside down before she allows us to occupy a bed in the hospital. I am sure you guys want to keep your limbs intact.'

Bertie had bestowed the moniker Cruella DeVille, after the vamp in the film *101 Dalmatians*, on Manisha. In fact, anyone who crossed his path was given a nickname. Singularly, he had achieved the feat of naming all the tormentors in our squadron. The monikers ranged from the Biblical ones like Cain, Herod, and Judas, to the more modern ones like Doctor No, Dracula, and Mogambo.

With just thirty rupees as allowance, we were always broke. The Gole Market shops, with their shelves bursting with exotic things drew wistful sighs, as we cycled by them. All we could afford was an occasional fag. The only cadets who had some money were the ones who had stuffed their pockets from home. In our group, Randy and Bertie were the moneyed guys. Randy's brother, a captain in the infantry, gave him fancy things and enough money to keep him smoking expensive brands through the term.

In Bertie's case, it was his mother who spoilt him. She laboured under the illusion that like every other hostel, the Academy supplied inedible food. The poor lady believed that her beloved son was next to starving, so she smuggled all the money she could into Bertie's wallet, right under his father's nose. Our pal didn't make any efforts at dispelling his mother's illusions. Rather, he worked on her emotions to extract more money.

Maachh and I were mostly pinned by the merciless talons of bankruptcy. After buying bare necessities like shaving cream and blades, soaps and toothpastes, nothing much remained in our wallets. I cursed the shaving habit imposed on us by the seniors, since it took a big bite of my small allowance.

With our emaciated wallets, all we could do on our Sunday trips to the city was stare longingly at the shop windows and the fancy restaurants. It was only when Randy or Bertie decided to open the purse strings that we sponged on them for an ice cream or a movie. Of course, I kept an impeccable account of the expenses in the fond hope that I would be able to return the borrowed amount one day.

Khare was a local chap. Come Sunday and his family would turn up at the squadron laden with homemade snacks. Academy rules specified that visitors could only be entertained in the anteroom. One day, the sight of Khare's mother with the packets of food was too much to bear. As soon as the dutiful son left the anteroom to see his folks off, we sped in and polished off everything.

When he returned after waving to his family, the poor man found nothing left, not even little scraps of the delicacies. After that day, Khare went out to meet his parents in the parking lot, finished the eats in the car, and then brought them to the anteroom.

Girls were an obsession with the cadets. One day, we discovered the photograph of a beautiful girl in Macchh's wallet.

'You scoundrel!' Bertie scolded him. 'Who is the girl residing in your wallet?'

'Oh, that! She is my girlfriend, Reena,' replied the Fish in a breezy manner.

'You mean you have a girlfriend, too?' We were incredulous. Which girl would want to befriend the Fish?

To prove his point, Maachh began to inscribe her name on the wristband of his watch. He also wrote it on his wrist in very small, barely noticeable letters.

'Just for motivation,' he explained.

Bertie was the next one to follow suit. He wrote 'Diana' on his wrist. We had no way of knowing whether he meant Phantom's girlfriend or his own.

Soon, the craze caught on among the other first-termers of G squadron. Every cadet displayed a female name on his wrist. Finding myself the odd one out, I wrote the name 'Sunita' although I didn't have a girlfriend. I suspect most of the first-termers didn't. Initially, the names were restricted to the wrist, and were written in small letters, which were generally not visible from a distance. With time, they began appearing on various parts of the body, and got washed off during the bath. As days passed, many of us got bolder and began writing the names in bigger letters and permanent ink.

It was around this time that the name of Manisha, the lady doctor who was a favourite with most cadets, appeared on the inner side of Harry's biceps. He wrote her name in big letters in permanent ink. One morning, during the PT parade, Captain Sabharwal caught sight of it when Harry was hanging from the beam. 'Come here you scoundrel. What is this?' he asked, pointing at the name.

Harry had been adventurous enough to use coloured ink to inscribe the name.

'Who is this Manisha?' barked Sabby. There was pin-drop silence as we waited for the reply. Seconds ticked by, and silence grew thicker.

'I am asking you a question, cadet, and I want a reply.'

Harry mumbled something incoherent that drove Sabby up the wall.

'Meet me in my office after PT,' Sabharwal announced angrily.

God knows what happened thereafter, but Harry was found scrubbing his biceps so hard that they became badly scarred. Permanent ink doesn't rub off easily.

The craze died as suddenly as it had begun.

'That bloody ***!' cursed our pal, his arms raw and swollen. 'All I had done was write a name. I didn't rape anyone.'

'That Sabby is a frustrated goon,' we all expressed our sympathies.

'Was Sabby born old?' asked Maachh indignantly.

'Why?'

'He doesn't understand the surge of testu... whatever,' he broke off.

'Testosterone,' I completed it for him.

'Boys of our age must be allowed some liberty,' the Fish frowned, 'I drew oodles of inspiration from the tattoo, and now he has taken it away.'

'Right! It certainly provided us the extra josh (energy), needed to carry us through the tough routine. Now, even that motivation has been snatched away from us,' Randy rued.

SEVEN

It was the month of festivals, and also the time for the mid-term break. Like a carbonated drink to which a pinch of salt has been added, our excitement seemed to froth over. The very thought of getting away from the Academy for four full days pepped up everyone. Most of the cadets were going home for the break. For the cadets from far-flung places like Assam and Jammu, it was an impossibility to go home for the brief period. But even they decided to get away from the Academy. Some of them went to stay with their local guardians in Poona, while some embarked on sightseeing trips to the south, or to Goa. A few, like us, were undecided about their plans.

In the afternoon, Maachh burst into my room and announced, 'Hey guys, did you know that the Academy has organized a trip to Bombay?'

'Fantastic! I would love to go there. Imagine – beaches, babes and beer!' sighed Randy.

'I am thinking of opting for the trip,' I said. 'There is no point going home for four days when two days would be wasted on the journey. Besides, I have never been to Bombay.'

My words elicited varied reactions from the gang.

'Hey man, our Pessi is getting adventurous!' shouted Bertie. 'What a transformation!'

'I will also opt for Bombay,' declared Maachh. 'If I go home, my dad is going to harass me about my grades. He expects me to take home a couple of trophies.'

Randy had no alternative but to go to Bombay since his parents were on a vacation to the Andaman Islands.

Since the three of us were opting for the Bombay trip, Bertie was reluctant to go home to Goa. That evening, when he called home to inform his parents about his change of plan, his mother began sobbing into the phone. He came back fuming. 'No luck! I've to go back to good ole Goa,' he confided. 'My mom uses emotional blackmail the way the army uses rocket launchers. Wonder what she'll do when I have to fight wars.'

In the end, it was Maachh, Randy and I who reached the shores of Bombay. The navy, our hosts, had made excellent arrangements for the cadets. After the tough routine we followed at the Academy, the break was like a five-star holiday, and we were determined to make the most of it.

Every day was a new day, packed with excitement and adventure. Not willing to lose a moment, we set out for exploration much before the city began stirring. We went to movies, and window-shopped to our hearts' content. We packed in as much bird watching in our schedule as possible, basked in the sun, and frolicked in the sand.

'This is life,' remarked Maachh, glancing around. We were lolling on the Juhu beach, close to the Sun 'n' Sand Hotel. From our vantage point, we could observe a few foreigners clad in the skimpiest bikinis we had ever seen. Our eyes popped out of their sockets when one of them removed her bra to tan herself.

'Boy, this is too much.' Maachh's excitement had reached a

feverish pitch.

'My dear *Fish*, this is Bombay,' laughed Randy. 'Don't forget we've to get back to the Academy.'

'Dampener!' retorted our pal. 'And I thought only Pessi was capable of it.'

The navy did its best to keep us occupied. I guess our host did not want the cadets to go berserk in Bombay, which we did anyway, at the first available opportunity. We were taken to the first aircraft carrier *INS Vikrant*, and shown around. With so many aircraft tucked in its belly, the entire ship looked like an impressive airport on the move. We were a privileged bunch to visit the first submarine acquired by India. It was a thrilling experience.

We visited most of the five-star hotels around the Gateway of India, parading confidently in the lobbies, and in the shopping arcades of the hotels. We loafed around as if we owned the place. By now, we had learnt to dress up immaculately and conduct ourselves smartly with a large dollop of self-confidence, although our pockets were empty. The hotel malls were too expensive, and all we could do was feast our eyes on the pricey ware displayed in its windows. We did, of course, indulge ourselves with a cup of coffee at the coffee bars. The luxurious surroundings made us feel like royalty.

'We could have had a feast elsewhere for the money we've paid for a single cup of coffee,' Maachh cribbed, as usual. 'What an utter waste.'

'It is not for the coffee you are paying, buddy, it is for the entire ambience,' commented Randy.

'I have made a decision,' I told the gang. 'I am coming back here to spend a night.'

We were seated in the lobby of Hotel Oberoi, in which a single room for a night cost more than what most people earned in a month. They threw me an incredulous look.

'Alone or with a girl?' Maachh asked.

'The first time will be solo.'

'And how do you intend paying for it?

'I did not say I am coming back tomorrow. I will come here when I get my first salary.'

'That makes sense.'

After a thoughtful minute, Randy spoke up. 'Let's make a pact. All of us will come back for a night at this hotel when we get our first pay packet, and we will have a blast.'

We shook hands on the pact, happy at the prospect of sharing fun at the hotel, at a later date.

The naval mess at Colaba was quite impressive. The ambience was as good as any upmarket hotel. It provided a glimpse of the life that awaited us after we got our commission. The thought of the promise of the future did a lot to cheer us up.

The trip was more enjoyable than we had expected. Unlike bad times, the good times roll away quickly. The days glided away too fast for our liking, and we braced ourselves to face the challenges that awaited us back at the Academy.

We landed back at around noon at the Academy. There was an entire evening to ourselves before we got back into the rut of Academy routine.

In the evening, Bertie returned with his suitcase bursting with cakes, pastries, sausages, and lots of goodies. My favourite was the homemade chicken pickle that his mother had thoughtfully packed for him.

'My mom went berserk when she saw me,' he informed us while unpacking his bags. 'According to my dear mater, I have lost a lot of weight. And boy, did she try to fatten me up in the forty-eight hours I was there!'

'Good for us,' said Maachh, sampling a sausage. 'Bertie boy, you have done a great turn for your pals by bringing all this stuff.'

'Wait till you see the special package,' he said, conjuring up a bottle from the bottom of his suitcase. 'This is the famous Goan feni. The treat is on me.'

'Bertie boy, please thank your mother for all this when you speak to her next. She's serving the nation, literally.' Randy fingered the bottle fondly.

'By the way, all of you have an open invitation at my place,' said Bertie. 'My mom found all of you underweight.'

He had taken home a picture of the four of us standing on the battle tank.

'It's the haircut that makes us look like that thin and hungry as if we have just arrived from Ethiopia,' said Maachh.

'Didn't your mom comment on the hair cut?' Maachh continued.

'She failed to recognize me at first, and then started crying. When I asked her why she was crying, she said it was my hair. It makes me look like a convict serving a sentence,' laughed Bertie. 'I guess it is quite an apt description.'

'Let's go to the Gole Market,' I suggested.

We exchanged notes about our trip, as we cycled down to the market. When we told him all about the beaches and the babes, and the coffee in the five-star hotel, Bertie cursed us loudly.

'You morons! You had all the fun, while I had to put up with my sobbing mom.'

The Gole Market was almost deserted. Most of the cadets had not yet returned from the break. The atmosphere was relaxed, and we felt on top of the world as we pedalled around the shopping area at leisure.

'Look at that!' Bertie exclaimed pointing towards a female.

'What?' asked Maachh, as he peered in all directions but the right one.

'That female, damn it! Pretty, isn't she?'

'Wow! She is really cute,' echoed Maachh.

'Not my type,' I commented, feigning boredom.

'Who asked you, anyway?'

There was no stopping Bertie now. He headed straight for the gift shop where the female was busy selecting a gift.

I tried to hold him back. 'Bertie,' I cautioned. 'I would be cautious if I were you. This is inside the campus, and you never know who she is. You might get into trouble.'

'I am just going to say hello to her!'

No one else said a word. I was the only one firing warning salvos.

Before Bertie could enter the shop, the female emerged from it, and halted near the parking lot. She spent a few minutes rummaging through her bag, and then reversed into the gift shop. Obviously, she had forgotten something.

'I am going to follow her,' Bertie was waiting with his bike.

'Let's not stand right in front of the shop; it will alert her,' said Maachh. 'We can wait under the tree at the other end. The moment she starts moving, we can tail her.'

'Look, I saw Captain Sabharwal's scooter in the parking lot. There will be trouble if he sees us,' I warned again.

'Pessi, stop being such a dampener. Sabby is nowhere here,' retorted Randy. 'I have checked all the shops.'

Since there were just about half a dozen shops, it was not difficult to locate someone like Sabby. But then, why was his scooter parked there, I wondered.

The lady was still inside the shop. I had half a mind to leave Maachh, Bertie, and Randy, to their fate. Tailing a female inside the campus could prove to be dangerous.

'Please carry on with your misadventure,' I told them. 'I am going back to the squadron.'

'Cautious Carl,' teased Bertie.

Leaving them sniggering behind my back, I entered a shop, bought soap and toothpaste, and went over to the parking area.

As I was pulling out my bike, I saw the female heading my

way. She said hello to me before pulling out Captain Sabharwal's scooter from the parking lot. Minutes later, she drove off. Warning bells began pealing loudly in my mind. In the meantime, Bertie and the rest of the gang were gathered under a distant tree at the other end.

I cursed. It was obvious that she was related to Sabby. It spelt trouble. There was no way I could warn the gang, who had already begun tailing the female.

I gathered the rest of the story when they returned, flustered from their escapade.

'Back so soon?' I addressed Bertie as he ran towards his room.

'Pessi, my dear chap, it was a very dangerous situation.' He was panting. 'Lucky you dropped out.'

'But what happened?'

'We tailed her up to the staff quarters successfully. Not once did she look back. Then she halted in front of Sabby's house.'

'And you guys were still on her tail?' I couldn't believe their stupidity.

'Maachh was sure that she couldn't be Sabby's relative. She must have borrowed his scooter, he kept saying. We hid ourselves behind the tall hedge and watched.'

At this juncture, Maachh arrived, huffing and puffing like an obsolete coal engine.

'Pessi, you *** baboon!' he began. 'Why didn't you warn us?'

This was absolutely intolerable. How could he accuse me of not warning them when I had been doing just that during the entire episode?

'You idiot! Did I speak in German or Japanese that you couldn't understand? What do you mean I didn't warn you?' I flared up.

I don't get angry easily, but there is no stopping me when I do.

'Cool it, Pessi,' Randy had joined us by now. 'You did warn us. It was stupid of us not to have heeded.'

Always the fair chap, Randy was a guy after my heart.

'Well, what happened after that?' I was curious to know the rest of the story.

'She honked twice, and Sabby emerged from the house. He greeted her saying "back so soon, darling?" And boy, did we scoot!' Randy let out a long sigh.

'And Maachh literally fell off his bike behind the hedge,' laughed Bertie. 'He couldn't believe she was Sabby's wife.'

'She looked so young,' Maachh defended himself. 'Who could have imagined that crusty fellow being married to such a pretty woman?'

'The moral of the story is: never follow a female without ascertaining her family tree,' I ended.

EIGHT

One evening, in the anteroom, all the first-termers were told to write articles for the NDA journal. There were just two stipulations: it had to be short, and it had to be related to the Academy.

We all knew that there was no room for so many articles from the first-termers in the NDA journal. With literary contributions flowing in from twelve squadrons, it would be impossible for the journal to accommodate all the budding Miltons and Shakespeares that populated the Academy. We calculated that only two articles from each squadron would find their way into print. Our SCC was an intellectual type, and he was sure to write a good piece. That would leave scope for only one more from the entire lot of us.

But orders are orders, especially in the Academy, and they can't be ignored. So we wrote stupid articles to complete the formality. Most of us were too lazy to put in the effort. Besides, where was the time for intellectual pursuit? The upside of the exercise was that the evenings at the anteroom promised to be entertaining, as each one of us was told to read our articles aloud.

Maachh vented his ire against the punishments he had received; Bertie penned his philosophy about the training; and Randy jotted down a few thoughts about his loneliness. I was in the process of churning my brain over a few pages on the magnificence of Indian army. The efforts, were mostly hilarious, and had the cadets rolling with laughter. Plainly, we were not cut out for a career in writing.

Harry wrote a howler about the cows, which entered the greens of the Academy from the dhobi ghat end, and caused havoc grazing and defecating all over the place. He opined that a small-scale enterprise for cow dung usage could benefit everyone.

Khare penned his views on the abolition of Sinhgad hikes and cross-country competitions. Ravi wanted athletes to be exempted from academic examinations. Rana went a step further. He penned a unique idea about allowing females into the Academy as cadets. All in all, the howlers provided fodder for laughter.

Only Srinivas Murthy, a studious kind, managed to pen a decent article on restrictions. It was titled 'Journey to Nowhere'.

His piece dealt with the daily evening run that a cadet punished with a 'restriction' had to undertake. Restriction involved wearing battle order dress, and running for about fifteen kilometres with a rifle, in stipulated time, while the other cadets were either playing games or relaxing. If he failed to finish it in time, he had to repeat the exercise. Murthy made the entire write- up quite poignant by pointing out tragic facts, including that the punished cadet, who returned totally exhausted and famished after the run, invariably discovered that tea had finished, and there were no snacks left, either.

Murthy went on to provide facts and figures to prove that with the amount of running a cadet did during his entire tenure at NDA, he could have run around the world. We weren't surprised when his article got selected for the journal, and he also bagged a prize for it. Murthy shot into the limelight and his articles were published in the journal each term till he passed out from the NDA. We knew he had an alternative career carved out for himself, were he to quit the Academy.

As the end of term exams approached, all ragging came to an abrupt halt. The cadets began slogging seriously. Maachh was the only one who seemed to remain unaffected.

'How does it matter, man?' he philosophized. 'All I want to do is pass. I am not aiming for a distinction. Besides, I have decided to cheat.'

Randy didn't burn the midnight oil either. Nor did Bertie. They laughed and jeered at me when I expressed my concern.

'Hey, Pessi, cram, man, cram!' laughed Bertie. 'Maybe I'll get lucky enough to sit behind you.'

While I learnt military history and geographical details by heart, they wrote small chits, and shoved them into the hemlines of their shorts.

'This is like taking a short cut during the cross-country run,' I told Maachh. 'Remember what happened when you tried to cheat?'

The tests came and went without creating a ripple of worry on their placid minds. I fretted and tensed up, while they sat for the tests, sneaked at their bits of chits, and came back laughing.

I wasn't surprised when Maachh just about scraped through the ordeal, with Randy giving him a small lead. Bertie made a smooth landing, thanks to his immaculate diagrams and neat notes.

As for me, I stood heads taller than all of them. I topped in maths as well as engineering drawing.

'Hard work always pays,' I repeated my father's oft-quoted words.

'You have to prove yourself to your father, we don't,' was the reply I got in return for my well-meant advice.

The first time I glimpsed envy in the eyes of my pals was when

I received the much-esteemed small badge with a star engraved on it. I strutted around the Academy with the badge pinned to my uniform pocket. I was now a torch holder. Torch holders were cadets who did well in academics.

'Pessi, you lucky dog! You are a hero,' declared Randy.

'Correction! Firstly, I am not a lucky dog, I am just a slogging dog versus you sleeping ones. Next, I am not a hero, but I have stopped being a zero.'

'I don't envy you the badge, but I do envy you the tea,' confessed Maachh. 'I have heard that the tea and snacks served at the commandant's bungalow are out of this world.'

'How I wish I had been able to cheat more effectively,' sighed Bertie.

Although I feigned nonchalance, my chest had puffed up by several inches. There was a look of grudging respect in the eyes of other cadets when I passed by. Even the seniors stopped abusing me.

The commandant gave away prizes to the toppers in each subject over dinner during a grand function at the mess.

The real significance of my badge dawned upon me when I was invited to tea by the commandant at his bungalow. It was customary for him to invite torch holders for tea, once every term. It was a very exclusive and prestigious event.

For the invitee cadets, it was a rare treat. The massive tables laden with the choicest snacks had the cadets drooling. In fact, for some cadets, the party was a motivating factor to do well in the exams.

For others, the party was the goal, regardless of whether they did well or not. One of these was Surjeet Gill, who was a glutton. He did not miss a party, whether he was invited or not.

'I will definitely go for the commandant's tea,' he declared, although he was far from being a torch holder. The thought of the delicacies served with the tea made him salivate.

'But the instructors know all the torch holders. You will only invite trouble for yourself if you walk in at the party,' the others warned.

For Gill, it was a challenge. 'Don't worry chaps, I'll manage them,' he assured us. 'I know all the tricks.'

He walked into the party confidently, along with the invitees. When an instructor of the science block questioned him, he told him that he had topped in English, and when an instructor of the Sudan Block confronted him, he said the award was for his engineering drawing. I admired the ease with which he sipped his tea and gorged on the snacks, while I stood sweating at his audacity.

Honours and medals were one thing, and being able to perform on stage, quite another. Even though I could manage a few awards in academics, I got cold feet when I went on stage. A small entertainment programme was held in every squadron at the end of each term. A few skits, songs, satires on the seniors, teachers, and officers, were the major attractions. Since the families of the senior officers, which included their daughters, were also expected to attend the show, the cadets vied with each other to capture the limelight.

Bertie and Maachh were exhibitionists. They liked nothing better than being on show. So when it was time for the end of term social, they volunteered to put up a skit.

Maachh came up with the brilliant idea of performing a 'Nagin (snake) dance' although he had two left feet.

'I could dress up like a female and do the contortions. It isn't too difficult to wriggle and writhe after all the front-rolling we have done.'

Everyone laughed at the thought of a moustachioed nagin, so the idea was dumped immediately.

In the end, Bertie and Maachh had to satisfy themselves with a hilarious impersonation of Captain Sabharwal, with gags about punishments. They managed to get a fair share of wolf whistles from the cadets who had suffered umpteen punishments awarded by the captain. Randy's skilful rendition of a hit tune on the harmonica brought him a lot of applause.

But it was Balwinder, with his peach-and-cream complexion, and long locks, who carried the day. The surd with delicate features dressed up as film star Mumtaz, and gyrated to a lusty cabaret number, bringing the house down. The whistles he generated were enough to set a record in the Guinness Book.

End of term also meant farewell time. The sixth-termers were on their way out after the three-year training. While it was good fun, a few rituals connected with the farewell made the event momentous. It was customary for the squadron officers and their wives to indulge in a mock fight with the seniors, in which they hit the sixth-termers with pillows, after the end of the programme. The mock fight was the harbinger of a more punitive practice. Trouble usually began after the departure of the officers. The sixth-termers were then left at the mercy of the juniors, who turned it into a night of revenge.

All through the term, the first-termers waited for the opportunity to settle scores with their tormentors. The end of term social was the only night when they found an opportunity to do so. The sixth-termers were given a sound thrashing and the CSM was a hunted man that night. After all the torture he had meted out to the juniors throughout the term, he was a prize catch on the farewell night.

Nowhere have I witnessed the use of such unique weapons for inflicting pain as during the send-off night. Towels became the tool to mete out punishment to the sixth-termers. This seemingly innocuous piece of fabric became a deadly instrument of torture in the hands of the juniors, who knotted one end of a towel, and used it as a whip on the buttocks. The more vicious cadets made it more lethal by hiding a lock inside the knotted end. The cracking power rose by notches with this simple improvisation.

The night of torture revealed the brutal side of the boys. Some sadistic cadets stubbed lighted fags on the faces of the sixthies, or subjected them to hot and cold baths till their bodies blistered. The toughies amongst the seniors were rounded up by the fifth-termers, given a thrashing, and passed downwards to the first-termers, with cadets from each term extracting their due.

It was a terrible time for the seniors, who got a dose of their own medicine from the juniors. The nicer ones among them got away with mild punishments, whereas the sadistic seniors were paid back in full, with compound interest.

The entire exercise was too violent for my liking; maybe I was soft.

'I think it is carrying things too far,' I remarked, walking down the corridor to escape the scene.

'They are getting as good as they gave. It is the law of natural justice,' replied Bertie, tying a knot in his towel.

'Don't worry, buddy, you'll also get it when you are in the sixth term,' warned Randy.

'Not if I am a benign senior,' I retorted.

The first-termers had gone berserk. They were pulling hair, tearing clothes, slapping, and boxing, and if a sixth-termer resisted, it got even worse for him. The torture continued for a reasonably long time. A few sixth-termers who knew of the impending danger had vanished after the officers made their exit. Maachh assured me that no one got away. Those who had run away would eventually be rounded up and teased for cowardice.

Most seniors faced the agony in a dignified manner. For those who managed to avoid the social and its aftermath, a disaster waited inside their cabin. Buckets of water were poured into their rooms through the ventilators to ruin their beds and possessions, rounding off the day for revenge.

NINE

Excitement began building up amongst the first-termers as the much-awaited Passing Out Parade preparations began. We had seen enough of it as visitors, and in documentaries and films, but it was the first time we would be participating in one.

For me, it held a special appeal. It was while attending a POP at the age of ten, awed by the magnificence of the entire event, that I had decided to join the Academy.

The euphoria dissipated as we went through innumerable rehearsals.The drudgery of endless marches to the commands and to the playing of the band, as we stomped our feet continuously, soon became a big pain.

'I have decided, enough is enough. No more rehearsals for me,' declared Bertie one evening.

'But the parades have to be attended,' I interjected.

'Not if one is sick,' he reminded me. 'I am reporting sick tomorrow morning.'

'Have you forgotten Manisha's torture?'

'I haven't,' he smiled. 'But Cruella's torture can't be worse than the parade rehearsals.'

'You are right, yaar.' Maachh, who had been intently studying the horizon for a silver lining, spoke up. 'I think I will go with you. Let us leave Randy and Pessi to represent us.'

So, the next morning, the two of them walked to the MI room, leaving us to stomp our feet. God knows what ailment they produced, but Bertie managed to charm the ice-block doc, and they were allowed to skip the rehearsals for a day.

'This isn't fair,' ranted Randy. 'Let us do it by turns. The two of you go for the rehearsals tomorrow, and I will report sick.'

'Suit yourself,' Bertie sniggered.

Randy reported sick with imaginary diarrhoea, while I pretended to be seized with terrible stomach spasms. Lady Cruella threw us a disdainful look that could have frozen all living creatures into immobility, and proceeded to dispense her vindictive medicine. I can only presume that Manisha didn't like the looks of us because she prescribed some laxative for me saying, 'If the pain persists, it could be your appendix, in which case, we'll resort to surgery.'

For Randy, it was a medicine that he swore tasted like diesel, which she insisted he take in front of her.

'I guess you must have eaten something that didn't agree with you,' she told him. 'If this doesn't work, I'll put you on the drip.'

The world looked a bleak and cruel place after we had finished with the MI room.

'Let us continue to stomp our feet on the parade ground,' Randy decided. 'It is a far safer place than Cruella's dispensary.'

The POP was as grand as I had remembered it to be. For the sixth-termers, it was a poignant affair. Many of the outgoing cadets, including those who were considered toughies, got emotional and broke down. Each of them had hordes of memories cached in their hearts and minds. They had transformed from gangly teenagers to strapping adults during the six terms at the Academy, in which time, the course mates had grown to be more important than the family. The tough life of the Academy had knitted a bond as vital as blood relations. Many of them would not meet again as they went to different academies for further training: the army cadets to the Indian Military Academy (IMA); the air force ones to the Air Force one; and the naval ones to yet another Academy.

All around us was a tragic atmosphere as the sniffling cadets went around hugging each other after the parade. Ahuja, a sixth-termer sat crying while his father and brother waited in the car. His mother sat by his side, moist-eyed, trying to console him.

'It is a highly melodramatic scene, man,' commented Maachh. 'I would give my left arm to escape from this hellhole. Here, these guys are getting an opportunity to flee, and yet they are weeping. I don't understand it at all.'

'It is one of nature's ironies,' I tried to explain. 'When you can't get away, you want to; and when they let you go, you just don't want to any more.'

'Another one of life's mysteries, I guess,' added Bertie.

Four buses and two army trucks were lined up at the mess to take the cadets and their baggage to the railway station. My heart filled with joy as I boarded the Academy bus.

'Four full weeks, imagine!' exclaimed Bertie. 'What a long parole!'

'And the best news is that we will be second-termers when we return to the Academy after the four-week break.' Maachh was ecstatic.

Most of us were taking the NDA special, which was a train meant exclusively for cadets going back home after the Passing Out Parade. Randy and I were taking the one that went to Delhi, while Maachh travelled by the one that headed eastward. Bertie decided to take the overnight bus to Goa.

A train full of boisterous boys with combat training could spell serious trouble for the stations they passed through. It was to ward off such calamities that the Academy sent the deadliest of the ustaads on the train with an express order to keep the cadets in control. A few semesters back, some cadets had bashed up a vendor for charging extra money. Although the errant cadets were subsequently caught and punished, the damage was done. The NDA special had earned its share of notoriety.

The moment our train arrived at the platform, the stalls lining the platforms downed their shutters, and all vendors vanished into thin air. The cadets were like animals let loose from the zoo. They needed no introduction. The 'katori' cut hairstyle left no one in doubt about our identity.

Every basket of eggs contains a couple of bad ones and so did the NDA special. These bad eggs behaved like goons from third-rate Hindi movies. They pounced on the stray vendors who dared to remain on the platform, bullying and terrorizing them.

The ustaads did not punish anyone in public. All they did was note the names of the offending cadets, and details of the offence committed by them. The offence, time and the place were noted in a meticulous manner, language notwithstanding. Scores would be settled once the cadets returned to the Academy for the next term. Each time the train stopped at a station, the ustaads dismounted from their compartments, and kept a watchful eye on the cadets. They were the only ones we were scared of.

Our seniors, who were old hands at travelling on the NDA special, knew all the tricks of the trade. As soon as the train chugged to a station, they would wear a cap to hide the 'gobri' haircut, sport their dark glasses, and venture out on the platform. Randy decided to follow suit.

Donning a pair of dark glasses and a cap, he sauntered along the platform. He demanded a cup of tea from the solitary tea vendor, and sipped it with great relish, his eyes focused on the signal. As soon as the train whistled, he finished his tea, and began walking away. When the vendor asked for money, he lifted his cap, and ran his hand over his scalp meaningfully. Revealing his 'gobri' cut was meant to indicate that he was from the special train, but the vendor was an old hand. He pointed at Ustaad Waryam Singh, who, anticipating trouble, had already begun walking towards them.

Randy quickly paid up and vanished into the nearest compartment before Waryam Singh could catch up with him.

The journey on the NDA special is an exciting experience. We played cards, cracked jokes, pulled pranks on each other, and time melted away silently as did the distance. Those who wanted to grab some sleep were packed off to the upper berths. Randy played the mouth organ all the time, drawing curses from some unmusical chaps. Nights were tussle time as the bookworms kept the lights on while the others, intent on grabbing some sleep, kept putting them off.

As time passed, the cadets grew restless. The novelty of the journey had worn off and everyone wanted to reach home.

Dawn was breaking when the train reached my destination. I was flooded with a sense of homecoming as soon as I alighted at the familiar station. The well-known sounds and smells made me feel emotional.

I had not informed my parents about the visit because I wanted to give them a surprise. And what a surprise they got when they saw me for the first time with my 'katori' cut! The rigorous exercises had melted all the fat I had carried on my body to the Academy. A couple of inches added to my height in the past few months, gave an extra edge to my personality. Most importantly, it was the impressive timbre of my voice that caught attention. From the teenage squeak, it had transformed into a deep masculine tone.

As mothers are wont to do, mine too lamented about my skinniness.

'Don't they feed you properly at the Academy?' was her first question after which she embarked on Operation Fattening.

'You won't believe how much I can eat,' I reassured her, and proceeded to demolish single-handedly a dozen slices of bread, and a couple of omelettes at the table, to prove my point.

All talk veered around the Academy for the next few days. I skipped the details about ragging, and tried to make life sound quite pleasant. For the first few days, I did nothing but eat and sleep. Everyone treated me like royalty. Even my father dropped all hostility to share man-to-man chats with me. I even managed to surprise my mom by making my own bed and putting my room in order.

People flooded me with curious questions wherever I went. Everyone wanted to know about the Academy, our training and the life there. My friends remarked about my personality, athletic build, and height that had shot up by four inches. I basked under the glow of the attention that came my way.

Public attention turns even the most restrained people into braggarts, and I was but a mere mortal. The picture I painted of the Academy was rosier by many degrees than the original. One secret I shared with no one, not even my mother, was the fact that I had contemplated running away from the NDA at one point of time.

As all good things come to an end, so did the break, and I was ready to leave for the Academy once more. Surprisingly, I was raring to get back. Amidst a string of sermons and cautions delivered by my parents, and weighed down by the big bag full of eatables, I embarked on the journey back to the Academy.

TEN

The daylong return journey to Poona provided me enough time to introspect. Lying on the upper berth of a thankfully less crowded compartment gave me an opportunity to think about the six months I had spent at the Academy. The 180 days had passed in a trice, but we had done much growing up. A smile creased my face at the recollection of the pranks we had played, and the eccentricity of each of my pals. Undeniably, we had suffered harsh punishments, but the days had been interspersed with moments of immense joy, too. I was still musing over the past six months when the train chugged into the Poona station.

The reception committee at the railway station packed us off in the bus and the truck, which took us straight to the mess. The sixth-term office holders, and the first-termers, had already arrived two days before us, a mandatory process. Breakfast was being served when we arrived at the mess. I was dying to meet my gang.

A little bit of hunting revealed the gang at the breakfast table, doing justice to the fare laid before them. Maachh and Randy greeted me like a brother lost in the Kumbh Mela. Both of them were sporting freshly grown moustaches.

Nothing had changed at the squadron, yet there were many small differences. We were at an age when transformations take place pretty rapidly. The embarrassing crack in the voice had disappeared for most first-termers, giving way to a more masculine tone. The most pleasing part was that most of us had grown way taller than we were when we had left. Some seemed to have shot up like Jack's beanstalk. Many of my course mates returned sporting a moustache, and had grown their hair as much as four weeks of pampering could allow.

The tapeworm was at work tucking in the repast with gusto. 'Life is good, man,' Maachh said, polishing off the double-egg omelette with half a dozen toasts. 'I was kind of getting Academy-sick. It's nice to be back.'

'The best part is that we are second-termers now, and we have the license to rag,' said Randy, rubbing his hands in anticipation.

All our course mates had the same thought running through their minds as we stepped out of the mess, fortified with the sumptuous meal.

There was just one problem. To rag a first-termer, we had to locate one. We couldn't spot a single fresher. They had probably finished their breakfast and returned to the squadrons under the watchful eyes of the sixth-termers.

'We have to be careful before we resort to any ragging,' I cautioned. 'What if we mistake a sixth-termer for a fresher?'

There was substance in my prudence. The Academy is too big a place to know all the cadets in one single term, and there is hardly any physical difference between the first- and the sixth-termers. There had been instances when we were mistaken for first-termers and hauled up by seniors who were also hunting for first-termers to rag.

'It's sort of frustrating not being able to lay our hands on a freshie,' Maachh's voice sounded regretful.

'Don't worry, there is plenty of time for getting at them,' consoled Randy. 'Let's get back to our squadron and catch hold of some first-termers on home ground.'

The moment we arrived at the squadron, we spotted nineteen first-termers hanging from the seventh heaven. Makhija, a fifth-term sergeant, was now the CSM. Though a terror for the juniors, he was considered a fair guy with an intellectual bent of mind. The moment he saw us entering the squadron, he let off some first-termers so that we could use them to get our rooms cleaned, and have our share of fun ragging them for the first time.

What is my name? What is my term? We swooped down like vultures on the sacrificial lambs, and blasted them with our artillery. Evidently, they didn't know our names, and said we were sixth-termers. Smart chaps! They knew that it made a junior feel happy if he was told that he was a sixth-termer. Once they had curried favour, the punishment was sure to be diluted.

'Hey, let's first check our cabin allocation,' said Randy. 'Then we can use the service of these piddly fellows to do them up.' We had already passed on our 'piddly' title to the freshers.

Each term, we were allotted a new set of cabins, and the list was displayed on the notice board in the centre lobby of the ground floor. A number of crosses and amendments had already been made on the list.

'Look, your cabin is at one end of the corridor, mine at another, and Maachh is nowhere around!' exclaimed Randy. 'I don't spot Bertie and Natty's name on our side of the floor, either.'

'What gross injustice! This won't do,' surmised Maachh, craning his long neck to get a good look at the list. 'We've got to hang around together.'

'Right you are,' I joined them. 'The four of us can't be strewn all over the second floor. Birds of a feather have to flock together. We can't go against nature.'

At times such as these, Randy proved to be most resourceful. He sauntered up to the CSM, and offered him a fag from his brand new pack of 555, which he had brought with him. After they had exchanged pleasantries, opined about the new crop of cadets, dissected the atmosphere at the Academy, and indulged in some loose talk with Randy cracking a few vulgar jokes, they got down to business.

Randy expressed his anguish at being separated from his pals, and wondered if Makhija could help him out. The softening up worked, and soon Randy was striding towards us wearing an elated expression.

'Don't worry, the problem has been sorted out. We are in adjacent cabins, so get cracking, and get the slaves to work,' he announced like a pharaoh.

We rounded a few first-termers to bring our luggage from the box room and do up the rooms. While the first-termers unpacked and did up our rooms, we sat in my room and exchanged notes about the four weeks away from the Academy. Our mouths worked overtime as we tried to speak and feast simultaneously on the snacks packed by our mothers.

The first-termers employed to do up our rooms needed constant supervision. Each one of us strutted over in turn, and reprimanded them over some silly mistake.

'They are taking too long to do the job. I guess it is time for them to taste some punishment,' said Randy, striding out importantly. We could hear him roaring at them. 'You call this cleaning? I will make you eat all the dirt you leave in the room.'

It seemed like a rerun of our humiliating days, except for the fact that we were not at the receiving end this time. He sent one of them packing, with orders to change into battle dress, for not having dusted his room properly.

'Get back in sixty seconds,' he commanded.

The fellow was smart. He disappeared. With so many new faces swarming around, there was no way of tracing him. 'If I lay my hands on the guy, he's had it,' fumed Randy.

We realized that even ragging required experience. Lesson learnt, we punished the remaining first-termers by asking them to front-roll or climb up to the seventh heaven. We were not letting them out of sight! Maachh even managed to evolve a new punishment: 'Climb up to the seventh heaven,' he barked. 'Climb up the strands of wire one by one while you are hanging.'

A couple of minutes later came the announcement that all first-termers were to go to the Quarter Master Store to collect their kits.

'This isn't fair,' ranted Maachh. 'We've hardly begun ragging.'

I was feeling quite benign towards the poor chaps. 'Have a heart,' I said. 'They will be back. We can get hold of them after lunch.'

Becoming second-termers doesn't elevate you to a hallowed position, we learnt soon enough. With no first-termers around, our seniors picked on us to run their errands, much to our chagrin.

As soon as lunch was over, we pounced on the first-termers. Since it was a holiday, the seniors were having their afternoon siesta, and we ran the place. And boy, did we cash in on the opportunity!

All the first-termers were as confused as we had been on our first day at the Academy. The bewildered lot sweated under our instructions. At tea-time, Randy caught a cadet, who had latched on to a senior, and made him crawl under the mat in the central corridor, just the way we had been made to do on our first day at the Academy.

By now, Bertie and Natty had also returned to the squadron. Happily they joined forces. 'There's got to be some benefit of being a second-termer,' said Bertie, as he commanded a first-termer to do some push-ups.

After a count of thirty, the chap couldn't do any more. He fell flat on his face and lay still. 'Don't ***mother earth!' shouted Bertie, drawing a large grin from his prey.

'You find that funny, eh?' Bertie hollered. 'Wait till I wipe that smirk off your face.'

He then proceeded to make the guy go through an agonizing round of 'Puttie Parade'. That really wiped the smile off the cadet's face.

While we were punishing the freshers, Giri, a fifth-termer, passed us by. He noticed Maachh's recently grown drooping moustache, and walked up to our pal.

'You ***ass don't you know that cadets are not supposed to sport a drooping moochh? Go and shave it off immediately!' he ordered.

All this was done in front of the first-termers whom Maachh was trying to bully. It was a humiliating moment, as the freshers tried to control their pleased grins. Maachh was furious.

'I am not going to forget this embarrassment,' he vowed. 'Watch out, Giri. I am going to make you pay for it,' Maachh said, behind the fifth-termer's back.

It was time for the evening tea. We saw a waiter from the mess arriving with tea and snacks. He was carrying a huge tray full of pastries. Maachh began drooling at the sight. 'I say, this is a rare treat. We must have done something good to deserve pastries with tea. I am going to feast on someone's share today,' he declared resolutely.

'Look, it is not going to work. Just take your share and be happy about it,' I warned.

'Like hell I will. Just watch it, buddy. I have got a brilliant idea.'

By now, we knew all about his brilliant ideas and their results. I sighed resignedly.

'Come here, you moron! Do you know my name and my

term?' He had caught hold of a first-termer and asked his questions belligerently.

The poor chap had no inkling.

After ordering him to execute a few front-rolls for the offence, Maachh continued, 'I am Giri, fifth term. Now go and get my share of pastries, and be snappy about it.'

We threw him a horrified look. Such a reckless act could only invite trouble, but our pal continued to grin. 'Don't worry, Pessi,' he soothed me. 'I just saw Giri going out of the squadron. By the time he returns, his share of pastries will be safely tucked in my tummy.'

The first-termer went and fetched tea and pastries without any difficulty. The trick worked, and Maachh was exhilarated. He had extracted the price for having to shave off his moustache.

The eats were kept in the CQMS's room. The rules were simple: the juniors who were running errands for the fifth- and sixth-termers, had to give the name and take the snacks. Elated with the success of his idea, Maachh went on to have the share of three sixth-termers that evening. What happened after the sixth-termers returned is anyone's guess.

As in the first term, the routine was gruelling. The only difference was that we were used to it by now, and went about it in a mechanical manner. And so, there was less stress. The civilian orderlies knew their job, and we were entirely dependent on them. So great was the dependence that most of us could not trace our wallets, handkerchiefs, and wrist watches, without their help. They did all the dusting and cleaning, arranged the books on the table, stitched buttons, and performed odd jobs for us. Our cabins were so similar in layout that it was difficult to differentiate between them. After an exhausting day, none of the cadets looked at the cabin number. We would barge into wrong rooms, especially during the beginning of the term. It was only when we looked at the timepiece on the table that we recognized our rooms, because that was the only object that differed.

Going to Poona on liberty was a big craze. With our wallets bursting with money after the break, we were dying to splurge. It was only after the breaks that we were rich; the rest of the term saw us in abject state of penury.

'Let's go for a movie, and round off the day with a grand meal,' suggested Bertie. There was not a single voice of dissent. With the 500 bucks nestling neatly in my wallet, I had no objection to their plans.

As luck would have it, Maachh and I were refused liberty after a minor scrape with a senior. We had walked into the cabin of a sixth-termer after a drill and sullied his room with our perspiring bodies. The guy got furious at this minor misdemeanour, and ordered us to clean his room instead of going to the city on liberty.

'You guys go ahead,' I said, a martyred look clouding my face.

'Don't be idiotic. Either the four of us go, or no one goes,' declared Randy.

There is something about the Academy that makes everyone take the word 'camaraderie' a bit too seriously. Randy's sacrifice touched me.

'I really don't mind,' I insisted.

'I do,' Maachh intervened. 'He is right. Either the lot of us goes, or no one does. It could happen the other way round next time. Wouldn't you do the same in that case?'

I knew I would. It wasn't for nothing that they called me Gandhi.

'But, how do we go?'

'Where there is a will... and all that crap, remember? I have a plan.' Maachh whispered conspiratorially.

'Oh, no!' the objection was unanimous. We didn't need Maachh's plans. He would manage to screw up everything.

'If we went according to your plans, we would never get a single liberty during the six terms we spend here,' said Bertie.

'This time, it is foolproof, man. Just listen to me.'

Resignedly, we decided to give him a hearing.

'We could sneak out to the main road through the dhobi ghat.'

His suggestion immediately drew vehement objection from Bertie. 'Are you crazy, man? The dhobi ghat is crawling with stray dogs.' He was mortally scared of the canine variety ever since he had been bitten by a frisky pup at the age of six.

He was right. Going out was easy, but returning to the Academy would be tough. After dark, the dogs in the adjoining village as well as the dhobi ghat, couldn't differentiate between a thief and a cadet. Quite often, truant cadets were bitten by dogs, while returning after a sojourn in the city. It was another matter that no one from Golf squadron had ever been bitten by a dog. The reason was probably the proximity of the G squadron to the dhobi ghat, or maybe the dogs recognized the cadets belonging to our squadron.

'The city is fifteen whole kilometres away,' I protested. Those not granted liberty were not allowed to travel by the NDA bus going to the city, which meant that we would have to walk or hitchhike.

'Okay, for Bertie it is the dogs, and for you the distance, right?' Maachh asked. 'You guys are absolutely piddly. No adventurism at all.'

'There is no word like adventurism,' commented Bertie.

'You bet there is. I know for sure.' Maachh was at his argumentative best.

'Cool it, man! Don't digress from the topic.' Randy, the umpire spoke up. 'I will take care of the dogs; I have a way with them.'

He would. I believed him. He could charm all living things, girls included.

'And who will handle the ustaads prowling around?' I asked.

Maachh's idea was by no means unique. It was a frequently tried and tested one. Cadets who didn't get liberty would often hazard their way through the dhobi ghat, and the ustaads lying in wait at the other end promptly brought them back.

We wore old clothes and dark glasses, but the haircut was a sure giveaway, so we all wore caps. That didn't help much, as the ustaads specially targeted guys with caps. Barely had we stepped near the periphery of the dhobi ghat circumventing all troubles when Ustaad Pyare Lal loomed in the distance. He spotted the four of us, and began running towards us.

'Nonsense, cadet, tham (stop)!' he roared.

His words propelled us into a faster gait. We knew that our goose was cooked if we were caught. Most likely, we would be punished severely and disallowed liberty for the rest of the term.

'Run!' shouted Maachh, leaping over the low wall that surrounded the dhobi ghat. We drew our caps low over our brows and sprinted like rabbits with the ustaad in hot pursuit. The distance and speed made it difficult for him to recognize us. We knew we were safe as long as he couldn't pinpoint our identity.

The Academy had made us smart and swift. We could outrun any ustaad, climb any wall, and break through any ambush. Soon, the four of us had gained a good lead, and Pyare Lal fell back, shaking his fist threateningly at us.

The day spent at the city was all the more enjoyable because of the sense of victory after the escape. The movie, meal, and the bird watching were worth all the trouble and more.

TN Swami, Tabby for short, a sixth-termer during our second term, was a great character. His room was in a constant state of disorder. The seniors would get after juniors to clean up, but he was a senior, and the boss. Every morning, he would emerge from his room virtually in his undies, and by the time he reached the ground floor, he would be fully dressed, picking things from the rooms of juniors, on his way down.

As the word about his activities spread, the juniors began avoiding him, and would leave their rooms well before Tabby emerged from his room. When the guy found that the juniors had locked their rooms and left, he began raiding his course mates' rooms.

One morning, we found him all black and blue after he came out from the bathing stall. We presumed that he had had a fall. Then we noticed that he had sobered down a lot and had also shed the habit of picking things from others' rooms. Everyone was relieved. It was much later that we learnt that his own course mates had thrashed Swami for his habits.

ELEVEN

The buzz was strong. A new deputy commandant had been posted to the Academy.

When Commodore Ferreira, who looked, thought and acted like Rommel, took over from his army counterpart, the cadets were delighted because, it was believed, that unlike their army counterparts, the navy chaps were a lenient lot.

Our happiness was short-lived. Ferreira proved to be a man wilier than the desert fox, and soon he had earned the label 'Ferreira the Führer', courtesy Bertie. Although we had yet to meet him, we had heard enough tales about him to warrant caution.

One morning, at dawn, while it was still dark, we were assembling in the squadron parade ground. It was usually first- to third-termers who came down first, followed by the fourth- and fifth-termers. The sixth-termers never came to the squadron parade ground, but went straight to classes from their cabins.

At dot 6.00 a.m., a voice barked in the dark, 'Stand where you are.' The voice was stern in inflection, loud in tenor, and impeccable in its accent. We stood rooted to the spot. The next moment, the headlights of a black Ambassador car, which was parked behind the bushes, were switched on, and Commodore Ferreira emerged from it.

'Where is your SCC?' he demanded. 'I mean, your ex-SCC.' He had already pronounced the punishment for the SCC.

On hearing his booming voice, the sixth-termers came running down. Like a one-man court, he dished out punishments to the seniors. He ticked them off for their late arrival, and generally shot off a series of punishments to a couple of sixth-termers who were not properly turned out.

For the juniors, it was a delightful morning. Any person who punished the seniors was a man to be respected. We were happy to see him sorting out the sixth-termers.

The moment the SCC came down, he was ordered to remove his shoulder tabs. Ferreira de-tabbed the SCC, and took away the tabs with him.

After the shock treatment, the Fü hrer began walking around the squads, inspecting the cadets. As Ferreira continued his inspection, tragedy struck Maachh. He didn't have his bike. Swami, who had a flat tyre, had taken his bike away.

'What is your bike number, son?' Ferreira asked Macchh.

'107, sir,' replied the Tragedy King.

The wily deputy went towards the rear of the squad where the sixth-termers were standing and spotted bike number 107.

Swami was awarded '28 plus 4', which meant that his entire month was booked; twenty-eight days of running, and four Sundays of the Sinhgad hike. One day more of the same punishment would amount to relegation (losing a term). From that day onwards, the sixth-termers knew they had met their match. There was a palpable smell of fear in the air.

During the second period, Ferreira landed up at the swimming pool, where the sixth-termers had assembled for their swimming class. He called the G squadron cadets to attention, and displayed the SCC shoulder tabs he had acquired in the morning. Even as the chaps were wondering about his intentions, he said, 'Anybody wants these?'

A few hands went up. Everybody wanted to be the SCC, certainly a prestigious appointment.

'Dive from the ten-metre board and it's yours,' the Fü hrer shouted.

The hands that had shot up a moment back were promptly withdrawn from sight. To jump from the ten-metre board was a tough task.

'No one?' he roared.

There was a silence thick enough to be cut with a butter knife. After a pause the Fü hrer shouted once more. 'Up you go, the whole lot of you, and dive from the ten-metre board. Scared of diving, are you?'

He made all the sixth-termers of G squadron jump six times each from the ten-metre board. The cadets trembled, not because of the height, but because of the devil in the form of Ferreira standing down below.

IP Singh, or Inky, who hesitated the least and proved to be a good diver, was awarded the tabs of the SCC.

During the same period, we were informed that we had a new SCC.

Maachh was thrilled. Now on, no senior ventured to take his bike. Before that fateful day, his bike had routinely found its way to a senior's hand. As a result, he had to go running to classes most mornings. At the same time, he had never seen a sixth-termer walk to classes.

'***rascals!'' he ranted. 'They never walk. I am going to make them run.'

He decided to deflate the tyres of the sixth-termers' bikes, targeting those he wanted to extract revenge from.

'What's the point in deflating their tyres when they can easily fill them up again?' I asked. 'Have you forgotten the bicycle-pump lying at the cycle stand?'

'Do you think I am as silly as that? If I deflated the tyres at night, and they discovered them in the morning, it will be too late for them to do anything. Lingering around will make them late for class. Besides, I am going to hide the pump, too.'

The first time Maachh tried to puncture a bike at night, it made such a loud hissing sound that all cabin windows overlooking the cycle park flung open, and he was caught red-handed. He got a sound thrashing and spent the entire night doing Puttie Parade. That put an end to another one of his brilliant ideas.

Many of the second-termers had brought exotic things from home. Since most of us had begun shaving just six months back, the desire to own expensive shaving creams, and aftershave lotions, was almost obsessive. As an unwritten law, just Old Spice was permitted to the junior lot. Only the sixth-termers had the privilege of using exotic brands of aftershave lotions. One evening, as we entered the anteroom, our nostrils perked up to the pleasant smell pervading the hall. The scent was overpowering and special. It was quite evident that it was an imported aftershave lotion, and an expensive one, too.

'Someone's got rich,' commented Maachh.

'Sshhh... could be a sixth-termer,' I cautioned.

Everyone was silent because no one knew who had used the aftershave, or which brand it was.

The moment the CSM arrived, he asked, 'Any females around?'

A heavy silence greeted his query. He continued, 'May I know who is trying to impress someone and whom?'

There was pin-drop silence as we sat like the deaf and mute.

'I am really impressed, and now I want to know by whom. Who is it? Own up.' He asked.

A first-termer, Irshad Hussain, tentatively raised his hand, and all heads turned towards him.

'I pity the poor pig,' muttered Maachh. 'He's going to buy it today.'

No first-termer had ever defied the unwritten rule.

'What's the brand?' the CSM asked Hussain.

'Brut, sir.'

'Go, get it.'

The poor chap doubled up to his room and brought the aftershave. It was immediately confiscated by the CSM. Thereafter, the CSM smelt of Brut whenever he went to the city on liberty.

The habit of confiscating expensive things wasn't restricted to the CSM. Most of the seniors never missed an opportunity to grab whatever came their way. Bertie's cousin was in the merchant navy, and he brought expensive chocolates, clothes, and perfumes regularly for his kin. The guy had just returned from a long voyage when Bertie went home for the break. We were astounded to see the articles our pal brought with him when he came back from the break. Like a true mate, he gifted each of us something from his collection. For Randy, there was a pack of expensive fags; for Maachh, a cologne; and for me, a smart silk tie.

We decided to smoke in Randy's room that night. Just as we had begun smoking, in walked a sixth-termer who had smelt the tobacco while passing through the corridor. He had run out of fags, and wanted to borrow some. In return, he was willing to overlook our offence. Smoking in the Academy was banned even for sixth-termers. It was a different matter that they flouted orders and smoked openly inside the squadron – what applied to them didn't apply to anyone else. If ever a junior was discovered smoking, the fellow would be punished severely, but it was considered the exclusive privilege of the sixth- termers to smoke in the squadron. The others had to smoke on the sly.

'If you lend me some fags, I can forgive you for the offence,' he blackmailed us.

Randy had kept a special pack just for such occasions. It was a Marlborough packet with cheaper fags inside. 'Take as many as you want, sir,' he offered magnanimously.

The senior was thrilled at the sight of the expensive pack. He nodded his head approvingly, and asked. 'Can I keep the whole pack?'

Randy winked at us behind the senior's back, and replied with a straight face, 'Of course, sir. It is all yours.'

No sooner had he left that we doubled up with laughter.

Randy loved smoking. In fact, he was quite addicted to the habit. The guy smoked nothing less than 555, but when the seniors came to borrow from him, he offered them Charminar, packed in expensive packets. It had helped him to establish a bond with the sixth-termers. Smoking a good brand was considered a status symbol. It was the packet cover that mattered, so most sixth-termers kept cheaper brand fags in exclusive packets, and flaunted them around to impress others. At the same time, when they ran short of fags, they didn't hesitate to borrow bidis from the civilian orderlies.

Our schedule was crammed with studies, exercises, and learning. The second term was worse because new skills were introduced in our busy routine. One of them was swimming. While the cadets who were from Sainik School knew swimming, there were a few like me who had never ventured near a pool. Of the twenty-two second-termers in the G squadron, there were six of us who had never entered water before.

The night before our swimming classes, I was a worried guy. No amount of reassurance from the gang could console me.

'You guys will not understand,' I cried. 'I suffer from hydrophobia. There is no way I can learn swimming.'

'Come on, Pessi. You've got to give it a shot,' said Bertie.

'We'll be there in the pool with you.'

'Yeah, the ustaads won't allow you to drown and sully the pool, so you are in no danger,' smirked Maachh.

The next morning, I stood shivering near the pool, staring at my reflection in the clear blue water. Tentatively, I stepped into the shallow end with the five non-swimmers, while the rest of my pals enjoyed themselves at the deep end. Gradually, the fear ebbed, and the six of us splashed around at the shallow end like little children. The first day ended quite pleasantly.

The next day was real bad. Ustaad Bahadur Thapa ordered the six of us to enter the deep waters. We looked aghast. How could we enter the deep waters when we didn't know anything about swimming? I looked at the others for help, but they were as nonplussed as I.

The ustaads came at us with long poles and pushed us into the deep end. My fervent pleas drew no sympathy from them. I spluttered and swallowed litres of water. I have never prayed as hard as I did at that moment, sincerely invoking all the deities I could think of. The thought that I would meet my watery grave so far away from home made me absolutely miserable.

In desperation I tried to cling on to the ustaad's long pole, but he gave me a nasty shove and I fell into the water. Determined to cling on to the pole, I caught hold of it again and wouldn't let him shake me off. This time, the ustaad let go of his pole, and I went down with it. I struggled to rise up from the bottom where I had sunk with the pole, and managed to emerge spluttering. Having drunk a bellyful of water, I struck out blindly with my limbs, trying to keep myself afloat. I was panting and puffing with exertion and fright. My eyes were bloodshot, and my lungs were on fire as I tried to stop breathing, for fear of swallowing more water.

The wild flapping of the limbs worked, and I managed to surface. Clinging desperately to the railing, I tanked up oxygen. The moment I had caught my breath, the ustaad emerged from the shadows and pushed me into the deep end once again. I began paddling and striking with my limbs, just as I had seen the others do – anything to keep myself from going down.

The second day was spiced up by an interesting incident. After our swimming lessons, when we emerged from the changing rooms, we found Maachh missing. He was still sitting in the pool, half submerged in the shallow water. The guy refused to emerge from his watery refuge. While swimming, the Tragedy King's swimming trunk, with its loosened elastic waist band, had slipped to the bottom of the pool. Nude as the day he was born, he clung to the railing, with only his head above the water. The ustaad finally realized his predicament, and threw him a towel, which the fish wrapped around his torso, and emerged amid catcalls.

The NDA teaches you fast. It was a matter of staying alive and afloat. Rocky learnt to keep afloat the very first day. I learnt it the second day, and the rest of the non-swimmers learnt it within the next two days. Once we had learnt to keep ourselves buoyant in the water, we were taught the correct breathing techniques, and the arm and leg movements. To practise the breaststroke, we were made to lie on our bellies on the floor and simulate the movements. Keeping the hands and legs off the floor was a major effort. This exhausting exercise carried on for a long time. It was a punishment, which we could escape only by getting into the water and practising the strokes effectively.

Within a week, I was able to manage a few strokes, and was taken off the floor. Surprisingly, I began to enjoy swimming. My hydrophobia was a thing from the past, and I was filled with an ambition to master the breaststroke. Maybe my seriousness had something to do with the weightage this stroke was given during the end-of-the-term swimming test. The jump from the ten-metre board was, of course, another matter. I dreaded it just much as everyone else did. Ninety-nine per cent of the cadets never practised the jump from the ten-metre board.

Randy seemed to be the only guy who enjoyed diving from that height.

'Once you get down to it, the damn thing is quite simple,' he boasted.

'All you have to do is go up on to the board, stare straight, and keep walking till you fall into the water.'

It was this seemingly stupid suggestion that helped me when the time came for the dive.

Passing the swimming test was mandatory or one lost a term. Of all the fears, 'relegation' was the one the cadets dreaded the most. So, even the worst case of hydrophobia got cured within a few days. By the end of the second term, there was hardly any difference between a novice and a champion. Cadets who learnt swimming in the second term went on to become swimming record holders in the fifth and sixth terms.

TWELVE

'I wonder what they take us to be – Superman or Phantom? We are expected to be know-alls. Talk about great expectations,' cribbed Maachh. 'One can't be a good swimmer, boxer, rider, athlete, shooter, and yet be good in academics. Next, they will want us to sprout wings and fly in the sky.'

'And to think that I joined the NDA because I thought I wouldn't have to slog over my lessons,' rued Bertie.

'I don't understand why you guys are cribbing so much,' scolded Randy. 'I would love to be a Superman. If you had to learn all these skills elsewhere, you would land up paying through your nose. Do you know how much it costs to learn any of these things?'

'I couldn't be bothered,' retorted Bertie. 'Who wants to learn all this, anyway?'

'There is an easy explanation for all this. When you join the army and have to fight a war, how will you cross a river if there are no bridges on it?' I reasoned. 'That is why you have to learn swimming.'

'I guess I will have to spar with the enemy, and ride horses to the battle,' Bertie said sarcastically.

This particular exchange of thoughts was taking place after our first boxing lesson. That morning, during the PT period, we had been made to wear boxing gloves, and taught the techniques of boxing.

'Cadet, pack in some power behind your punch,' the instructor commanded, amused at my puny attempts. I convinced myself that the punching bag was a senior's face and that helped a little.

'I wish it was the ***CSM's face I was punching,' panted Maachh, landing a solid blow on his punching bag.

I guess most of the juniors were using the punching bag to release their frustration. Shadow boxing was a real howler, as each of us tried to spar with our shadows.

By the end of the practice, our arms were painful appendages.

'How I wish I could remove my arms and hang them somewhere,' moaned Bertie, massaging his biceps.

When a friendly third-termer overheard us complaining, he commented, 'You morons, stop cribbing about your aching arms! Wait till you begin riding. You will be complaining about your sore bottoms then.'

His words came true too soon. Within a couple of days, we found ourselves cycling towards the stables, which were located near the glider drome.

The only horses I had seen in my life were the ones seen during the marriage season, on which the dulhe raja (bridegroom) rode – probably, the same ones were used to pull tongas during the off season. But seeing a horse up close had a sobering effect, for one never knew when it may kick one. From close quarters, the horses seemed larger than the ones I had seen. They looked all the more daunting when you had to mount them without using stirrups. As usual, the Sainik School cadets were one up on the public school ones. Most of them were good riders.

Our first lesson began with an introduction to the horses and the saddlery. We were dressed up in our riding gear, which comprised riding breeches and a pith hat. Even the horses seemed to be accustomed to this particular dress. We were supposed to pat the horses and say 'shaabash ghoda (good horse)' thrice, to which the animals responded with a neigh, as though in acknowledgement of our appreciation. This drill seemed to establish a bond between the cadet and the horse.

On the first day, we were made to practise the art of mounting and dismounting the horse, after which we were let loose in a wooden enclosure with our steed. My horse, Gambhir, wore a philosophical look on its handsome face.

I was hesitant to mount my charger although it looked benign enough to allay my fears. Intending to establish a tighter bond, I patted it the specified number of times, and repeated the procedure again for good measure. Like a parrot, I kept repeating 'shaabash ghoda' nervously. Gambhir looked solemnly at me and neighed sympathetically. I got a feeling that it could read my predicament precisely.

'Dhyan de, cadet (Pay attention cadet)!' barked Ustaad Raghubir Singh, the tall and stalwart Rajput with a safa (turban) on his head. He looked formidable with his huge twirling moustache. 'Cadet, mount. Pehle canter karega phir trot (First you will canter and then trot),' he instructed.

The ustaads were experts, and many of them had won medals at national and international competitions.

I looked askance first at the ustaad and then at Gambhir. The ustaad took the lead, and the rest of us followed dutifully. The horses seemed to know their job very well. We didn't have to do anything because they followed the ustaad's horse in a disciplined manner. This was an exercise meant for the horse and the rider to get used to each other. Although I didn't seem to get used to the horse, Gambhir seemed to have got used to me. Maybe it sensed my nervousness, and responded with courtesy.

After a couple of rounds, the ustaad, satisfied with the progress of his cadets, shouted, 'Chaal badal (Change the pace).' It was an indication for the horses to begin trotting.

Gambhir seemed to understand the ustaad's commands better than I, and followed the horses without any effort from me.

Cadets who showed confidence in handling the horses after the first lesson, were taken out for cross-country riding, with the ustaad leading. I, however, continued to go round in circles within the safety of the wooden enclosure. From time to time, a couple of horses would return sans the rider, and that made me determined to continue trotting safely within the enclosure. Seeing the thrown rider limping behind as the squad returned to the stables, was a discomfiting experience.

One day, Randy's horse returned without him. As I craned my neck anxiously to catch a glimpse of him, he made his appearance, all dishevelled and bruised. For once, his tall figure had done the damage. He had been knocked off when his horse ran into a low branch.

Bertie was thrown off his steed when Toofan, his horse, bucked and reared. Such incidents were quite common in the beginning, but they managed to scare me. I tried to delay my cross-country ride as long as possible, till the ustaad got after me.

'Nonsense, cadet!' he shouted. 'Ghode par mount karega aur chalega (Mount the horse and move)!'

It was during the cross-country rides that the battle for the fattest or the slowest horse would begin. Tota, an oddly named horse, was the uncrowned king of sloth. No one remembered seeing Tota run or step up its pace despite all kinds of threats and cajoling. Like an enlightened one who has attained a fair degree of spirituality, the horse remained unruffled even during the most provocative situation. Kabutar, another enlightened soul, though not in Tota's class, maintained a calm disposition for most of his waking hours.

For those who wanted to avoid riding, Tota was the first choice, followed by Kabutar, and Mayur. I made a beeline for Tota, but there were two other second-termers fighting over the bemused horse. Ultimately, I had to settle for Kabutar, who turned out to be easier to ride than the fast and wilful ones like Gaddar and Toofan.

All second-termers dreaded riding Sher Khan, Gaddar and Toofan. These three horses formed a treacherous trio, with a penchant for kicking and bucking. Invariably, they ensured that their riders had a nasty fall. Only the best riders could return unscathed after riding them.

If a cadet had the misfortune of spoiling the ustaad's mood, he would be handed over one of the notorious horses as punishment. Bertie, who never refused a challenge, suffered under the illusion that he was an excellent rider, and accepted a wager for riding Toofan. That was when he was thrown off, and came limping back to the stables.

Although life had gone into the fourth gear for all of us, crowded as it was with different kinds of training and academics, whatever spare time we had was spent thinking about food and girls, in the reverse order.

Randy was a cool guy with a natural flair for attracting girls. He didn't have to bother about chasing them. They were attracted to him like goats to green grass. All he had to do was loll around the Gole Market, and he was sure to make a conquest.

Maachh was a loser. He could neither attract girls nor get them off his mind. The only girls he had ever conversed with were his sister's friends, and they talked to him more out of concern for his sister than his charm.

For Bertie, girls were a challenge. He would seek them out, act gallant with them, and press his luck. Though not a bad looker, his over-enthusiasm frightened the girls away. There was always an ongoing competition between Maachh and him where girls were concerned.

As for me, my nervousness with girls fetched me only solicitous and motherly attention. In school, I had been sought out by girls who wanted me to solve difficult mathematical problems, but I could never venture beyond the complex math problems. It had something to do with my childhood. Surrounded as I was by my domineering sisters, I found the female sex intimidating. Although I dreamt of having a steady girlfriend, gathering up courage to woo a girl remained a distant dream.

After our break, most cadets returned with photographs of smiling girls in their wallets. Everyone proclaimed them as photographs of their girlfriends, but most probably, they were just boasting. Very few cadets from the second term had any girlfriends, at least, not the steady kind who would give them photographs.

One evening, as we climbed into the tank, the conversation veered towards girlfriends. Maachh carried the photo of his girlfriend in his wallet, or so he claimed to our sceptical gang.

'How long have you known her?' asked Bertie, clearly jealous when he saw the beautiful, smiling girl in the picture.

'Oh, a long time now,' replied Maachh flippantly, as though he were a Casanova, and romantic affairs were routine for him.

'I don't believe you.'

'How does it matter whether you believe it or not?' Maachh retorted belligerently. 'I know what's going through your mind. You must be thinking that no girl would look at me, but the truth is somewhat different, my dear friend.'

The matter was getting out of hand, and Randy, as usual, had to intervene.

'Okay chaps, it is time to call a truce. One thing I want to make clear at this stage is that we should never squabble about girls.'

I seconded the proposal, and both of them made a solemn promise not to fight over girls.

Bertie and Maachh were forever on the prowl, seeking

females. They were ceaselessly working out ways and means of befriending them. The two seemed to be obsessed with the idea of introducing the flavour of romance in their barren lives.

Their favourite hunting ground was the Gole Market. The funniest part was that Bertie didn't want Maachh to accompany him during his forays there. 'It cramps my style,' he complained to me. 'No girl will look my way if that buffoon accompanies me.'

Frankly speaking, I found Bertie a nice and lovable chap. He was quite good-looking. Besides, he had a fantastic sense of humour. I liked the way his eyes crinkled up when he laughed, giving him a very impish look. The only department where he was a little lacking was height. But he more than made up for it with his attractive smile. He was loaded with charm, and full of chivalry. Besides, he was a terrific dancer, while Maachh had two left feet. Maybe being a Goan gave him these advantages. When it came to wooing a girl, he was far ahead of the poor Bong.

Bertie's hunting ground was restricted to the Gole Market, and his favourite haunt was the card shop, which was frequented by sentimental girls who picked up cards for all occasions. Like a gentleman, Bertie would leap to open the door for them, or perform some equally gallant action. His gestures were designed to melt the toughest of hearts. The only obstacle in his path was Maachh, who was always in tow.

One look at Maachh, and his gaping mouth, and the girls would make a quick exit. Not surprisingly, Bertie's first task was to shake off Maachh.

'I have to call my mom,' was his oft-repeated excuse. Thereafter, he would head in the direction of a public phone booth, leaving Maachh to do his window-shopping, and while Maachh unsuspectingly remained engrossed in the task, Bertie would sneak off in another direction. It was difficult to shake off the obstinate chap because Maachh was always a step behind.

Bertie realized that he would not be able to make any

headway as long as he was saddled with Maachh, so he hit upon an idea.

There was a small church within the campus, and Bertie decided to get devout. It was one place where, he was sure, Maachh wouldn't want to tag along. The next Sunday, dressed neatly in his mufti, and smelling of Old Spice, Bertie made his way to the church.

'Why has he suddenly turned religious?' wondered Maachh.

'Must be the tests looming in the distance,' I hazarded a guess.

'Not likely.' Maachh shook his head doubtfully. 'I know the guy inside out, down to his bone marrow. He is not the religious kind.'

He confronted Bertie immediately upon his return.

'Did Jesus listen to your prayers and throw some good-looking girl in your path?'

'Shut up,' replied Bertie, irritated with Maachh's questioning.

'Don't try to duck, man. We all know why you went to the church.'

'I am a Catholic, and my religion demands that I visit the church every Sunday. Anything wrong with that?'

'Nothing except that I don't believe the reason for your visit.'

'Who cares what you think?'

'It's okay, Bertie. What Maachh means is that one could do two things at a time. For instance, you could pray while concentrating on the girl seated in front of you,' Randy commented.

His remark diffused the strain. Randy was the unquestioned leader of the pack. He was a balanced guy, with the right mix of seriousness and light-heartedness.

The next Sunday, Bertie again made his way to the church, while we went to the city on liberty.

'I know he is up to no good,' Maachh was brimming with resentment. 'What kind of a pal is he to desert the gang?'

'Let him be,' said Randy. 'Why can't you leave him alone? He will come back when his mission is accomplished.'

Although disgruntled, Maachh held his tongue when he realized that both Randy and I were not in favour of interfering.

Three times in a row, Bertie did not come with us to the city. This was a serious turn of events.

'It is time we paid our homage to Jesus Christ,' said Randy. 'We'll tail Bertie when he goes to the church next Sunday.'

Maachh enthusiastically supported the suggestion. 'Yes, we must. We must see what the guy is up to.'

'Shouldn't we leave him alone?' I asked cautiously.

'Certainly not! He is a pal, isn't he? If he is in trouble, it is our duty to rescue him,' said Maachh, expressing his solidarity.

'According to you, he is tailing some girl, so how could he get into trouble?' I asked.

'Girls are the biggest trouble a guy could have,' he replied seriously.

Maachh was absolutely vehement about shadowing Bertie to the church. I could literally see him rubbing his hands gleefully in anticipation of catching him red-handed.

The next Sunday, the three of us began following Bertie from a respectful distance. We need not have bothered. The guy was so preoccupied that he didn't look back even once.

Silently, we slid into a pew at the back. From our vantage point, we watched our friend as he took his place in the second row, just behind a curly-haired damsel. Saner chaps than Bertie have fallen in love at the first sight of a pert nose, and a pair of mesmerizing eyes shining under a pair of arched brows; and this one even had a mole above her upper lip.

'Wow! I don't blame him for his recent conduct,' Maachh declared *sotto voce*.

The three of us stared appreciatively at the object of Bertie's fancy. She was worth relegation, we agreed. We slipped out of the church just as the service was getting over, and stood behind a clump of trees lining the path.

The crowd of Sunday worshippers began emerging after a while.

'What's Bulldog doing here?' whispered Maachh, pointing to the heavy-jowled man walking beside the curly-haired angel.

'He's also a Catholic,' reminded Randy, 'doing what every other Catholic in the campus is doing.'

The Bulldog, Mr Stephen D'Souza, our geography instructor was well known in the Academy. He was a temperamental chap, cool one instant, and hot the other.

'Oh man!' Randy slapped his forehead. 'The female is Bulldog's daughter!' Being in the vicinity of the church had definitely had an effect on Randy.

'Bertie has had it,' I commented.

The Bulldog was not known for his kindness. Besides, Bertie's performance in geography had been miserable. He couldn't differentiate between Australia and Russia on the world map. To his ignorant mind, Meghalaya was a part of Sikkim, and he never scored more than thirty-five in the subject, which just about got him through.

'Can't imagine Bulldog having such a pretty daughter,' sighed Maachh.

'He will rip Bertie apart if he gets to know of his interest in the daughter,' I predicted. 'He's not named Bulldog for nothing.'

'Let's get back,' Randy commanded. We had no intention of being caught by Bulldog. Besides, we had seen enough.

We picked up our cycles, and began pedalling furiously back to the squadron. The intention was to reach there before our pal.

After dinner, in our battle tank that night, Maachh cornered Bertie, 'Don't you want to stay in our group any longer?' he asked Bertie seriously.

'Where is the doubt, man?' Bertie replied.

'There shouldn't be secrets among friends, don't you agree?'

'There are no secrets,' replied Bertie, puzzled where the discussion was leading.

'Well, then, share with us the happenings at the church,' said Maachh. He looked at us for support, but we pretended to be deeply engrossed in our fags. Randy and I had decided to keep out of the discussion. We would step in only if things got hot.

Bertie was clearly not in a mood to share the details of his rendezvous with us. When the Fish's efforts at interrogation failed, Randy and I decided to get the truth out of him. Puffing on our fags stylishly, we embarked on the job.

'Bertie, wouldn't you like to share your experience with us?' began Randy. 'We are your pals, after all.'

No one dared to defy Randy when he took on that tone.

'Actually, there isn't much to share.' Bertie let out a ring of smoke through his nostril. He had perfected the art, much to Maachh's embarrassment, since he had been trying to blow the curly ribbons of smoke for a long time.

'He is not going to tell us,' declared Maachh, his nostrils flared with the effort of blowing smoke rings.

'We are waiting, Bertie,' Randy reminded gently.

'Okay. I will tell you all that happened,' the guy finally relented. 'The first time I went to church I happened to sit behind a lovely female. She was the best-looking girl I have ever seen.'

A dreamy look floated over Bertie's face.

'I waited for her to look back, which, of course, she didn't. At the end of the Mass, when everyone was moving out, I saw her father. He turned out to be our geography instructor, D'Souza. I was so upset with the discovery that I doubled back to the squadron without approaching her.'

'You fool!' swore Maachh. 'You should have gone up to Bulldog and wished him.'

'Do you really think I should approach the Bulldog?' Bertie

asked Randy.

'I think you should. Like cancer, he would either be benign or malignant. If he is benign, you can continue haunting the church, and his daughter, without any fear, but if he is malignant, stop the pursuit immediately. That's my advice.'

As usual, Randy's analysis made sense.

'Just think about it. The church is the ideal place for such an experiment. He couldn't tear you apart in a religious place, and that too, just after singing hymns,' I added my bit of wisdom.

The Sunday after that, we all decided to share the experience of Bertie's interaction with the Bulldog.

'It will boost my confidence,' he said, requesting our presence.

It would be a make or break affair. We decided to trade it for a morning of window-shopping in the city.

'Having you guys around will give me moral strength,' said Bertie.

'Don't worry, that's what buddies are for. We'll hide behind the nearest clump of trees and pray for your welfare,' I assured him.

'If you want us to cheer you, we'll do that,' Maachh added flippantly.

Concealed in the safety of the bushes, we waited for the Bulldog and others to emerge from the church after the Mass, which he did soon enough, smiling from cheek to cheek. His wife, a docile-looking woman, followed a step behind, with the daughter.

'He's in a good mood,' said Randy.

'Imagine the Bulldog smiling,' tittered Maachh, pleased with his comment. 'He must be a bully at home. Look at his timid wife and daughter.'

'Bulldog wouldn't be ferocious if he had a harridan for a wife,' I commented philosophically.

'Harridan! What's that?' asked Maachh, wanting to brush up his vocabulary.

'Don't bother, you wouldn't understand,' consoled Randy, patting his shoulder.

"There he comes,' shouted Maachh. Our pal had materialized.

Bertie, who was tailing the crowd, suddenly straightened his shoulders and approached the geography instructor. We could easily hear the two of them from our vantage point.

'Good morning, sir,' Bertie greeted the Bulldog politely.

'Good morning,' the Bulldog replied, his brows arching into a dangerous angle of irritation. He looked at our pal as though he were a toad that had hopped out of the pond right on to his bed. It was clear that Bertie's intrusion was not welcome.

The girl was watching the interaction intently.

'I am Cadet Albert Rebello, sir,' Bertie tried again. He was wiping his sweaty palms on the seat of his trousers. His feet were constantly shuffling, a sure giveaway of his nervousness. We felt sorry for the chap.

'Tcchhh,' sympathized Randy. 'All this humiliation just for a girl ...'

Randy was a complete male chauvinist.

'Oh, yes, you are in the second term, aren't you?' said the Bulldog sternly. 'I remember now. Your grades in geography are miserable, my son. Work harder on the subject instead of tailing your instructors.' His manner was as frosty as the weather in Antarctica. Our chum nodded his head dutifully, croaked out a reply, and moved out of the Bulldog's path. Bertie looked awfully crestfallen. It was downright mean of the Bulldog. We could imagine Bertie's position. Imagine being snubbed before the very girl you wanted to impress. Randy's face was the hue of a black storm as we rode back to the squadron. 'That guy hits below the belt,' he hissed.

It was a very glum Bertie who returned to the squadron later in the morning.

'It was your idea that I should wish the Bulldog.' He blamed us for the fallout. 'I should not have listened to you guys.'

'That idiot of a Bulldog,' raged Randy. 'How dare he insult you right in front of the church crowd?'

'Sorry, Bertie,' I apologized for the gang. 'We never thought he would turn out to be such a cad.'

'What's a cad?' Maachh intervened. 'Something like bad?'

'Never mind,' said Randy. 'You took a chance and it didn't work. That doesn't mean that you should get so dejected.'

Over dinner, a collective decision was made. The Bulldog needed to be taught a lesson.

Our minds were ticking furiously as we discussed various plans and discarded them. As usual Maachh came up with the most preposterous ideas.

Finally, it was decided that we would puncture his scooter tyres, for three days in a row. That would be revenge enough. Each of us was assigned the task of deflating the Bulldog's tyres on the designated days.

First, it was Randy's turn. He performed the job without any problem, while Maachh kept vigil. We need not have worried about being seen. If a cadet came across another one deflating an instructor's tyres, he would've been just too pleased. No one squealed on anyone, that was the first rule in the Academy – not even under extreme provocation. The seniors and the instructors were our sworn enemies.

A little while later, the pompous instructor arrived at the parking lot, and kicked his scooter to a start. Minutes later, he dismounted and stared at the deflated tyre. We watched gleefully from a distance, as the Bulldog walked his scooter home that afternoon, in the sweltering heat. Phase one of the operation had been carried out successfully.

It was my turn next. I did my bit without any hitch, and we watched again as the Bulldog stared disbelievingly at his scooter tyres, and cursed. He realized it was no accident. The tyre couldn't have developed another puncture the very next day.

It was on the third day, during Maachh's turn to puncture the tyres, that things went wrong. The Tragedy King, as usual, was on an overdrive. He decided to break the rear-view mirror as well. While he was in the act of extracting revenge, we spied the Bulldog arriving.

There was no time to warn our friend, who was busy hitting the mirror with a large stone. Maachh stood there for a moment admiring his handiwork when the Bulldog appeared round the bend. It took him an instant to understand what Maachh was doing, and he ran towards the parking lot, his face a furious crimson. The Bulldog began yelling at Maachh, who took off on his spindly legs on the double.

'Stop! Stop, you *** cadet!' shouted the Bulldog, running after him. 'Come here, this instant!'

But there was no stopping Maachh. Without a backward glance, he disappeared into the maze of classes in the Sudan Block.

The Bulldog hadn't been able to recognize our pal from the back. It was a close shave, and we heaved a sigh of relief. He reported the matter to the deputy who assured him that an investigation would be launched. For the next two weeks, the Bulldog left his scooter home and walked to the classes, sometimes taking a lift from another instructor. We had a tough time keeping a straight face each time we attended his class. The dirty looks he directed at us gave us a feeling that he knew who the culprits were, but had no proof to substantiate his suspicions.

Bertie returned from his next visit to the church grinning like a Cheshire cat, and performed a superb somersault right before us. He floated around the squadron perched on cloud nine.

'She spoke to me,' he waltzed around us with his imaginary partner.

'Tell us the details,' ordered Randy. The starry-eyed lover boy went on to pour the entire episode into our eager ears. 'I am happy that the Bulldog insulted me that day,' he said mysteriously. '... because it made Lizzie feel sorry for me. And guess what! She apologized for her father's boorish behaviour.'

'Really!' We were all agog. 'What else did she say?'

At that critical moment, our pal clammed up, and began floating like a friendly ghost around the squadron, greeting everyone with unprecedented zest.

'It is funny what a guy in love will do,' muttered Randy.

Mid-term break was round the corner, and there was excitement all around. Amidst the flurry of activities and preparations to go home, Bertie and his romance took a back seat.

THIRTEEN

The short mid-term break provided the breather we required after the fast-paced weeks of training. Barely had we settled down after the short respite when life shifted into a higher gear. It was time for Camp Greenhorn.

'This is what I joined NDA for,' exclaimed Maachh enthusiastically. 'Camps are the best thing about our training.'

Outdoor camps were held thrice during the six terms. In the second term it was Camp Greenhorn, Camp Rover in the fourth term, and Camp Torna, the toughest of the lot, in the sixth term.

We grew excited as the days for Camp Greenhorn neared. We were to stay out for a couple of days in tents in the vicinity of a village called Pirangut. More than anything, it was the thought that we would be out of the clutches of the seniors that made it all the more exciting.

We were in a boisterous mood as we pitched our 180-pounder tents on the slopes of a hill located about four kilometres from the village. The undulating hills, faraway forests, and the village lying beneath it, had a calming effect on our minds. There was no electricity or tap water, but we didn't care. It was exhilarating to rough it out in the open.

Since the tents housed eight cadets each, our gang, including Natty, had three second-termers for company. The first day was spent in hard labour as settling down was the first priority. Pitching the tents was a major task, and we were left with no energy to prowl around after the sun went down. Back inside the tent, we chatted about the coming day and its offers.

On the second night, we decided to go to the village after we finished the fifteen-kilometre night march. Even though we were totally exhausted after the long march, our enthusiasm for an escapade remained undiminished.

'We must taste the local brew,' said Bertie. 'The tharra (country liquor) is supposed to taste a bit like our Goan feni. And boy, does it have a kick!'

Maachh was terribly excited at the prospect of getting drunk. Till now we had experimented with smaller things like fags and bidis. Drinks were taboo in the Academy, even for the sixth-termers. Cautiously, armed with a torch, we slunk into the night and made our way down the hill towards the village.

Unfortunately, by the time we reached the village, only one country liquor shop was open. A few chaps in various stages of drunkenness sat on charpais (string cots). They threw curious looks at us. We decided to ignore the lot, and approached the counter, behind which sat a huge man. He looked intimidating.

'That guy looks like a villain from the Bollywood movies,' whispered Natty, his Adam's apple bobbing apprehensively. 'Are you guys sure you want to have the stuff?'

'Don't chicken out,' scolded Bertie. 'We have taken a decision and we will stick by it.'

'Look, there is no point in drinking the stuff here. After we get drunk, we may not be able to find our way back to the camp.' As usual, Randy offered sane advice.

'Besides, I don't like the look of the chap behind the counter. Once we are drunk, who knows what he would do!' I muttered under my breath.

'I have an idea,' said Maachh.

'Oh no, not another one,' said Bertie dramatically, striking his forehead with his hand.

'This time, it is a gem of an idea,' insisted Maachh.

'Okay, shoot.' said Randy.

'Let us go back now and return with our water bottles tomorrow night. We could carry back the tharra in the bottles and drink it peacefully inside the tent.'

For once, Maachh seemed to have an idea that appealed to everyone.

'Kya hai (What is it)?' roared the hulk behind the counter. 'Lena hai ki nahin (Do you want it or not)?'

'Kal lenge (We will take it tomorrow),' replied Randy briefly, and we beat a hasty retreat before the guy could come up with a rejoinder. Hooting laughter followed us till we turned around the corner into the next lane. Bertie seemed disappointed at the shelving of the plan. 'Wonder if we will be able to come back.'

'Don't worry,' consoled Natty. 'I have another idea.'

Till now, he had always been a satellite revolving around our gang, neither in it nor away from it. 'One of my Sainik School classmates mentioned that there is a girl called Batti in this village. She likes cadets.'

'How does your friend know about her?' Maachh asked suspiciously, his antenna shooting up.

'Most third-termers know about her. My friend, Anil, and his course mates visited her when they came here for a camp last year.'

'You mean she is a prostitute,' stated Randy.

'No yaar, she is not a prostitute in that sense. Let's call her an obliging female,' Natty replied. True to his nature, his vocabulary was also mild.

'Means the same thing,' I muttered.

'Well, I am game,' said Bertie. 'No harm in approaching her.'

'Okay, let's go,' Maachh agreed. 'Natty, kindly lead.'

'Anil has drawn a map for me. He said her digs are a kilometre from the village school. We'll have to locate the school first, and then work our way from there.'

Natty led the way and we followed him.

The moment we stepped into the dark lane, we were greeted by a couple of mangy dogs. They triggered their efficient alarm system, and were rewarded with an immediate response from their two dozen brethren scattered around the place. Getting braver, they began chasing us. It was nearing the witching hour and the entire village had gone to sleep. Not a soul could be seen on the streets. Save for the country liquor shop, all other shops had downed their shutters earlier in the evening.

Bertie was our leader as we beat a hasty retreat. Mortally afraid of stray dogs, he outclassed all of us in sprinting towards the exit of the village, followed by the four of us, with the barking curs in tow. A few lights came up in the windows as we deserted the village. Finally, the dogs fell back, and we paused for a breather outside the camp.

'Bloody unsuccessful mission,' lamented Maachh. 'First the country liquor, and then the girl. Nothing worked out.'

'Don't worry, we will come prepared tomorrow night,' comforted Randy.

Our entry and exit into the camp area was quite easy since we treated it as an enemy camp, and applied all the battle tactics we had learnt to avoid being caught. It was a challenge to get inside our tent undetected by the cadet on guard duty. During the camps, cadets manned the sentry post by turns. Even if the sentry on duty managed to catch us, he would let us off because the chap would most probably be going out himself when he was off duty. And one of us could be on duty the night he went out.

The next night, the five of us ventured out once again. This time, we carried Natty's water bottle with us.

The hoodlum at the counter threw us an amused look and asked: 'Kya bhai, phir aa gaye (So brother, you are back again)?'

We pushed Randy to the front. At six feet one inch, he was the tallest and most impressive. He towered over the guy and smiled tolerantly, 'Haan bhai phir aa gaye. Lekin aaj khalee haath nahin jayenge (Yes brother, we are back again. But today we'll not leave empty-handed from your shop).'

The guy seemed quite pleased with the reply, and offered us his best seats. Then he proceeded to point out his speciality, and eulogized the efficacy of each product. 'Pehli baar hai kya (Is it the first time)?' he asked.

Randy reluctantly admitted that it was the first time we would be sampling country liquor.

"To phir yeh theek rahega (Then this should be all right),' the chap stated, handing over a bottle. We could barely discern the contents in the dim light of the lantern.

Randy quickly grabbed the bottle, made the payment, and we scooted out of the shop followed by catcalls from the other customers. Once outside, we filled up the tharra in Natty's water bottle.

'What about Batti?' asked Maachh. 'Were we not supposed to find her house tonight?'

'Not tonight,' replied Bertie. 'Let us sample the tharra tonight. Trying out two new things could be too much for us,' he ended meaningfully.

So we abandoned our initial plan to hunt out Batti's house, and made our way back to the tent.

When we retuned to the camp, many of the cadets, dog-tired after the long and arduous march, had already gone to sleep. We could hear them snoring as we stealthily made our way into the tent. We entered the tent, sealed the flaps, put off the lamps, and slid into our beds. Bertie took out his shaded torch and opened the lid of the bottle. A burst of obnoxious and overpowering odour filled our noses. It spread quickly in the confines of the tent. He wrinkled his nose and took a valiant sip of the brew. Our friend then paused for effect, while the others watched him eagerly for any sign of drunkenness. Nothing happened to alter his disposition, so he took another swig with the arrogance of an ace, and passed the bottle to Randy. Randy feigned taking a big gulp and passed it to Natty. I was watching the entire performance closely. My observant eyes noticed that Randy had not swallowed the drink. Natty, in mock bravado, took two huge gulps and passed it to me. I hated the smell, so I also pretended to take a swig and passed it on to Maachh who was eagerly awaiting his turn.

'It doesn't taste half as bad as it smells,' he declared through a mouthful of the brew.

Meanwhile, Bertie declared that he was feeling tipsy. Natty wanted to puke. Everyone pretended to be tipsy. There was much play-acting as Rebello stood up, swaying, and fell heavily on his bed. One single bottle of liquor, which was still half full, and the whole lot of us were faking drunkenness. It was hilarious. The only guys who could be high were Natty and Maachh, because they had genuinely taken large swigs from the bottle.

The next morning at 5.00 a.m., when we got up, everyone seemed to be normal. After classes and breakfast, a long march was scheduled at 9.00 a.m. It was a hot day, and the sun smiled unrelentingly. Natty did not throw away the liquor from his bottle.

'We can't risk it. The stink will definitely attract attention, and we will get into trouble,' he whispered as we assembled in the open. 'I will carry it along, and the moment there is an opportunity, I will dump the contents in some field.'

Only those who have marched through a rough terrain, dressed in battle dress, with backpacks, will know what an ordeal it can be. Forget the heroes in movies who are shown as rough and tough guys enjoying their hikes. We were no Sylvester Stallones. With the sun beating down ferociously, a long march is anything but enjoyable. We literally had our tongues hanging out like dogs on a hot day. The moment a break was announced, we headed for the nearest shade, removed the backpacks, and lay down for a couple of minutes. Some of us even managed to catch a nap, and could be heard snoring.

The breaks were few and far in between, and too short for our liking. Captain Sabharwal, who was accompanying us, was not carrying a water bottle. During the breaks, he would pick up a cadet's bottle and drink from it. By noon, all the water bottles were empty, and our throats were parched like sandpaper.

During a break, Sabharwal began hunting for a water bottle with some water in it. After going through several empty ones, he spotted Natty's bottle, which was lying under a tree. He picked it up and shook it to check if it had water. It didn't seem empty. He opened it to take a sip, and the smell of the liquor hit him immediately. Normally a cool guy, he yelled as though he had been attacked by a swarm of bees. The bottle had Natty's number painted on it, so there was no doubt about the ownership of the bottle.

'You ***buffoons, you've been carrying liquor in your water bottle!' he ranted. 'Wait till we reach the camp. Get up, move!'

Sabby cut the break short, and ordered us to front-roll all the way to the camp. Natty drew fourteen days of restriction.

For once, Maachh was thrilled that the tragedy had not happened to him.

Natty's punishment put all our adventures into a spin. We had decided to visit the village by day, and follow the route given by Anil Bagaria to the girl 'Batti's' house. Unfortunately, after the punishment, our buddy had to spend all his free time under Ustaad Waryam Singh, who ensured that the cadets sweated copiously under his watchful eyes. Ever since he had heard the saying, 'The more you sweat in peace, the less you bleed in war', the ustaad had adopted it as his lifeline.

'Oh ***!' Bertie threw his cap on the bed, and stood staring at it for a moment. 'With Natty in a limbo, we can't venture out to the village. He is the only guy who knows the route to the girl's place.'

'After what happened that night, do you still want to venture into the village?' Randy joked, recollecting the chasing mongrels.

Bertie seemed cowed by the reference.

'Arre yaar, a couple of dogs shouldn't deter brave cadets,' said Maachh, thumping Bertie's back. 'Let us give it a try tonight.'

Somehow no one seemed interested. The fear of dogs, and Natty's punishment, had dampened our enthusiasm. Besides, all the marching had taken the wind off our sails. At the moment, the bed seemed more inviting than a girl's charms. In any case, time was running out. We were scheduled to move back to the Academy the next morning.

While we were busy trying our hands at different games and mastering none, Randy concentrated on his tennis. A player with potential, he was much in demand as a partner on the courts. So, the tennis court was his address on most evenings. There were five courts in the Academy, three of which were meant for the cadets, and the rest were reserved for the instructors and their families.

We were surprised when Natty bought a tennis racquet, for he did not know a tennis racquet from a cricket bat. More surprises awaited us when the next evening, Maachh landed up at the tennis court, brandishing his brand new racquet, which he held like a rifle. Soon, the courts were swamped with new entrants like Dhillon, Harsh, Kalra, Gill, Chowdhary, and Roopinder. Everyone wanted to play tennis although no one knew how.

We were surprised when cadets from other squadrons, who did not know how to hold a racquet, began arriving by the dozen.

From then on, on most evenings, one could spot a horde of cadets patiently waiting for their turn at the net. Tennis became the most popular game. The reason for the popularity of the game was not far to seek. The tennis courts were the only place where the cadets could meet the daughters of officers and civilian instructors. The short skirts and tight shirts were lure enough. Girls frequented the courts, probably for the same reasons as the cadets.

Randy's troubles began at the tennis court. Not one of the superfluous players, he was serious about his game, and concentrated on his backhand rather than the girls in the adjoining courts. But his dashing looks, muscular arms, and adept game, drew the girls like flies to a sugarcane-juicing machine.

'What is it about Randy that makes the girls swoon?' blurted Maachh. He had been unsuccessful in his bid to find a place near the net. I could enumerate a dozen points, but I controlled myself and replied straightfacedly, 'I guess it is his backhand.'

'Backhand! My foot!' Maachh fumed. 'I wish I could get a chance at the net. I could prove myself to be as good a player as any.'

'It is not just his play. Look at his biceps. They seem to move with a life of their own. The girls must find it real hot.' Bertie added fuel to fire as Maachh stole a glance at his own puny biceps. It was true. Randy was getting more handsome with each passing term.

I tried to suppress my smile. All of us knew how good Maachh was at his game. On the only occasion he had managed to have a go at the game, he had thrown the racquet instead of the ball.

'There are lots of other games in the Academy,' I consoled. 'Why don't you try swimming? You are pretty good at it.'

'I will! The day they allow females into the pool!' His voice dripped with venom.

In the meantime, Randy was making good progress in the game. As I sat watching his strong strokes and winning streak, I couldn't help noticing one attractive girl in the adjoining court who was desperately trying to catch his attention. Clad in a real short skirt, she bounced around, making the cadets drool. Her game was as bad as Maachh's. They would make a good pair, I thought. Randy, concentrating on his adversary's moves, failed to notice the girl.

The bait dangled tantalizingly each evening, with the skirt getting more provocative, and the shirt getting tighter. Our hearts thumping madly, we stared at her without blinking.

'She's waving at Randy,' exclaimed Bertie.

'And he refuses to notice her,' I added.

'Oh boy, I wish she would wave at me,' he sighed dramatically, his eyes enlarged to saucer dimensions.

'Play like Randy and she might.'

'I say guys, Randy's abnormal. Imagine! Not reacting to the attention of such a bomb!'

'If paying attention to your game is abnormal, then he is abnormal,' I defended Randy. 'Depends on what your priorities are.'

Bertie called out to Randy. 'Hey winner, look around. There are people waiting for your highness's royal attention.'

Randy was busy towelling off his sweat after the game, which he had won with a thumping score.

He casually looked around, and this time, he noticed the girl waving frantically at him. 'Oh, god, not again!' he swore under his breath.

'What happened?' I was curious at the expletives that dropped from his mouth.

'That girl has been hounding me for the past couple of weeks,' he muttered, waving back at her. 'She turns up at the court every evening, and tries to distract me from my game.'

'I thought that should please you,' said Bertie.

'No, yaar, she doesn't interest me.'

As we stood talking, she crossed the court and made her way towards us.

'Hi,' she smiled. What a smile it was! I was instantly floored. With a winning smile like that, one could floor the angels, but she hadn't made a dent in Randy's armour. I wondered why. Was he really abnormal as Bertie had diagnosed? Or was he being faithful to a steady girlfriend back home?

'I am Reema,' she paused for a reaction, which didn't seem forthcoming.

Bertie and I quickly extended our hands and introduced ourselves.

'And this is Randy... Randhir Singh,' I spoke for Randy, who seemed to have passed into the world of the deaf and mute.

The girl had her eyes trained on Randy, but the stupid man was studying his racquet with utmost concentration. 'You are too good. I wish I could play like you,' she ended lamely.

Randy had still not reacted. He seemed to have transcended into another realm.

'Will you teach me the backhand manoeuvre?' Her eyes were pleading.

'Well, thanks for your compliment.' Randy remembered his manners just as we thought he had forgotten them. He cleared his throat, and chose his words carefully, 'I am sorry I won't be able to show you the manoeuvre. I have a project to complete, so I am taking a break from tennis for a couple of weeks.'

Her sigh shook up our hearts. It came from the depth of her heart like a typhoon that had lost its way.

Bertie gaped at Randy as though he had taken leave of his senses. I thought it was time for me to arbitrate. It was necessary to console the girl.What if she broke into tears that were hovering dangerously around the rims of her eyes? She had not taken Randy's rejection lightly.

'Well, Reema,' I began. My voice trembled as though it was out on a mission to the Antarctic. 'Here is what we will do. Both Bertie and I will help him with his project so that he is able to return to the courts and teach you the backhand.'

'Thanks, you are such an understanding guy.' Her words suffused my body with warmth, and I felt I was sailing in mid-air. Afraid of falling down, I looked at my shoes, and the lump in my throat began tapping dangerously at my mouth. Not wanting to risk my heart leaping out of the ribcage, I bowed low and excused myself.

'What's wrong with you, man?' exclaimed Bertie, as we cycled back to the squadron.

'What's wrong with you guys?' Randy fielded.

'I mean, here is such a pretty girl, panting for you, and you treat her like dirt.'

'Do you know who she is?' asked Randy.

'No.' Bertie and I jointly claimed ignorance about the girl.

'She is Chopra's daughter. Now if any of you want to develop a friendship with her, you are welcome to it.'

Chopra was our physics instructor, as evil a man as could be. No cadet dared to cross his path. The guy was a demon. My ardour cooled off like ice poured on burning logs.

'For Reema, I would take on Satan if need be,' replied Bertie, his eyes lit up with reverence. 'She is worth hazaar (a thousand) battles.'

'Unfortunately, she won't look at you,' I reminded the guy cruelly. 'Besides, have you forgotten Lizzie?'

'That's the saddest part. Anyway, tell me why you can't take on Chopra. I have taken on the Bulldog, haven't I?' he asked Randy, his voice belligerent.

'I am not interested in her or any other girl here in the Academy.'

'You expect me to believe that?'

'That's up to you. All I regret is that I will have to miss out on the game for a few days.'

Maachh couldn't believe his ears when we told him about the

rejection episode.

'He's gone off his rocker,' he finally commented. 'If a girl like that approached me, I would jump from space without a parachute.'

It was an unusually quiet Randy who cycled with us towards classes one morning.

'What is keeping Randy boy quiet?' asked Bertie, who didn't like morose faces around.

'Yaar, Bats has awarded me three restrictions,' confided Randy.

Flight Lieutenant Arun Batra aka Bats was our divisional officer.

Normally a happy-go-lucky chap, Batra would get mad once in a while when things went wrong with his love life. Restriction was something that even the bravehearts resented. It involved running a specified distance every evening, dressed in full battle order with a dummy rifle, under the supervision of the ustaads. If one did not complete the run in time, the same had to be repeated. The timing was very stiff with no scope for a break in the run.

'But what did you do to earn the wrath of our beloved Div O?' I asked.

'It was the stupid bike inspection that caused all the trouble. The bike mechanic told Bats that my bike was all screwed up. According to him, the ball-bearing was gone, and there was a great deal of mud stuck to the bike. If I had known about the inspection, I would have cleaned it up,' Randy said.

It had rained the entire day, and cycling around had left a lot of muck sticking to all our bikes. The bike inspection was ill-timed.

'You are really a stupid guy. Should have left it standing in the rain all night,' I suggested.

'The idea didn't strike me,' Randy replied.

That night, as we went out to our favourite haunt for a fag, Randy spoke his mind.

'I think Bats is taking revenge,' he confessed.

I agreed. All the bikes were mired in dirt, yet he chose to punish Randy. 'Why would he do that?' I asked.

'I think he saw Reema waving at me at the tennis court that day'.

'So what?' Maachh interjected.

'Don't you know that the guy has been haunting the tennis court for her?'

'Et tu Brutus!' exclaimed Maachh, his penchant for misquoting playing up.

'No wonder the guy has been throwing deadly looks at you for the past few days.'

Batra was a bachelor on a constant prowl for female company. Like the cadets, he frequented the tennis courts to impress Reema. Unfortunately, Randy, unaware of his love interest, had beaten him in a few games.

'Go, tell him you are not interested in the girl,' prodded Bertie.

'Don't be silly. How can I tell him that?'

'Keep off the tennis court, buddy, that is the only remedy,' commented Maachh.

Randy had to bear with the punishment. He stopped playing tennis for a few months, during which Reema lost interest in him, and so did Batra. Whether Reema returned his interest or not we never found out, but Batra also stopped haunting the courts after a while. He had found a new love interest.

FOURTEEN

The Fü hrer wasn't getting any more popular with the cadets. His strictness, coupled with stringent punishments, was a sore point with cadets right from the first to the sixth term.

One Sunday morning, we decided to play cricket in the squadron parade ground. Since it was not a cricket ground, and there were no proper wickets, we improvised by using chairs for wickets, and hockey sticks for bats. The casualness of the game made it more exciting.

We were hard at our game when the deputy passed us on his rounds. He stopped his car and joined us in the game. Initially, we felt a little uncomfortable in his presence, but as he got involved in the game, we relaxed and began enjoying ourselves. He dropped all pretence and played the game on an equal footing.

Half an hour later, when he decided to leave, he called all of us, and in a grave voice, charged us for misuse of government property. It was improper to use chairs for wickets, he said.

This was rather underhand, we felt. Did he not realize that chairs were being used when he joined in to play?

Ghai, a third-termer, was a brave guy. He spoke up. 'Sir,' he said, 'you shared the fun so you should share the punishment, too.'

There was pin-drop silence as Ghai matched the deputy's stare without flinching. We waited for the flare-up that was likely to follow.

'What is the guy up to?' muttered Randy under his breath. 'He'll send us for a high jump.'

We were surprised at Ghai's audacity. The deputy seemed stumped by his reasoning. The resultant heaviness in the air seemed to drop like bricks on us. After a minute, the Fü hrer broke into loud guffaws. 'I love it, my boy. I love it!' he roared. 'What guts! I admire your nerve. What's your name, my boy?' he asked.

'Cadet Amit Ghai, sir.'

The Fü hrer thumped Ghai on his back, 'Carry on. Enjoy yourselves. Have a nice day,' he said, as he got into his car, with only his posture displaying the anger he felt.

When the Fü hrer left, we lifted Amit on our shoulders. He was a hero who had dared to take on the lion.

'You are one helluva gutsy guy,' Randy spoke for all of us. We all surrounded Ghai, and waited for his reply.

'Did I do anything wrong? It was just fair,' Ghai stated casually. 'It is known as the law of natural justice, buddies.'

Later, we got to know where his bravado came from. Ghai's father was a general in the army, and no one takes on a general, not even the Fü hrer.

We were now in the third term, and reasonably well adjusted to the problems in the Academy. Most of us were full-grown adults now. The passing time had also given us some maturity. We began to take things a little more seriously although there were some like Maachh who displayed no change.

Most cadets attached a lot of importance to badges and ranks. Wearing the lanyard had a special significance. It was an indicator that you were good at drill. To be allowed to wear a lanyard, we had to go through the 'drill square test', which simply meant that we had to bang our feet as hard as possible, creating as much din as we could. The awarding of the lanyard depended ninety-nine per cent on banging our feet to please the adjutant and the ustaad, with only one per cent as the luck factor. The harder we banged our feet, the better the chances of passing the test.

Hardly any cadet passed the drill square test in the first term. It required serious banging, which one got used to as time passed. Most cadets passed it in the second term, and the balance in the third. If a cadet didn't pass it in the third term, he could be relegated.

Maachh, with his casual attitude, had failed to pass the test in his first as well as the second term, while the rest of us had cleared it in our second term.

'Damn this banging,' he raged. 'I feel as though my brains are popping out of my skull.'

We didn't sympathize.

'Even if your brain becomes unhinged and begins to wobble all around your skull, you will have to continue the drill,' Randy declared ruthlessly.

'Have a heart, Randy,' begged Maachh. 'I really can feel my brain wobble when I bang my feet. I see stars by day each time I bang my feet, I swear.'

'We'll have to help this guy out,' said Randy. 'Without our help, there is no way he is going to clear the test.'

So we planned a double strategy to help out Maachh to clear his drill square test. On the one hand, we did our best to motivate the Bong and psyche him into packing all his power into his feet, while on the other, we put in some PR work on the ustaad.

'Ustaad, this time Mitra will definitely clear the drill. He has been practising very hard to clear the test,' Randy told the ustaad.

'He had better!' growled the burly Sikh, who was to judge

Maachh's performance.

To reinforce his point, Randy led the ustaad to the squadron parade ground where Maachh was busy torturing his feet, banging them hard on the ground. It was all planned, of course. Nevertheless, the sight of Macchh had the desired effect on the surprised ustaad.

'shaabash, cadet. Is baar pucca pass ho jayega (Well done, cadet, this time you will surely pass),' he declared with feeling. The sight of a cadet practising drill at the odd hour had touched his heartstrings.

And sure enough, Maachh cleared his test. It was celebration time inside the battle tank that evening. Bertie had brought some Goan feni on his last visit home. We all took tentative swigs from the bottle and the effect of the brew was noticeable. I turned philosophical, Randy got sentimental, and Maachh turned into a laughing machine, while Bertie began lamenting loudly about the missing hatch of the battle tank.

'Thhish is a serious matter' he slurred. 'Whoooshh stolen the damn thing?'

'Not I,' Maachh tittered. 'It is Randy, I am sure.'

'Even if he's stolen it, he can't escape from the clutches of his conscience,' I sermonized. 'Randy, my brother,' I continued. 'it is better to exist with a clear conscience than to live with the stolen hatch.'

'I knew it,' Randy began, 'I knew you guys would backstab me one day.'

It was Natty who finally reminded us that we had a bed in the squadron and it was awaiting our arrival.

'Damn the bed, Nath,' said Bertie. 'If Randy had ssshhtolen the bed, I wouldn't mind. But a hatch of a captured enemy battle tank isshh a different matter.'

The moon had crossed over to the other side when we finally hit our beds.

In the first term we were unsure, groping and insecure and the ragging had taken the wind out of us. The second term was marked by a casual and carefree attitude. We had got used to the gruelling lifestyle, and adjusted to the seniors' demands. The beginning of the third term was breezy, but after we returned from the mid-term break, a competitive attitude began to surface. The third term was marked with all-round competitions, be it games or academics. There was a challenge at every step, and one had to prove oneself. Life had begun turning serious.

Each competition brought out the squadron spirit in the Academy. Camaraderie and the competitive spirit bubbled like champagne. During the competitions, the entire squadron turned up at the grounds, and the cadets yelled their guts out for their favourites. Although we had come to the third term, the seniors still remained detested enemies. During the boxing competition, if the participant was a sixth-term appointee, the entire Academy would cheer against him. The greatest excitement was when a second-termer was pitted against a sixth-termer. Everyone cheered the junior, and if, by chance, the sixth-termer lost to the second-termer, it was considered highly disgraceful, and the senior had no option but to go into hibernation.

Although the four of us had kept away from all competitive sports, it was by default that I got to participate in one. Inter-squadron boxing competitions were held every term, and the participants treated like royalty. They got a lot of privileges like extra food, early bed, and excused fall-ins, besides the 'no punishments' benefit.

Towards the end of the term, a bout was arranged with a cadet in the same weight category. This was known as 'novices boxing'. Although I harboured no ambitions of a pugilistic career, I was pitted against a sardar called Dhillon. Frankly speaking, I was terrified of sharing the ring with my opponent who sported a thick beard, and had a lot of hair on his body. His ursine appearance had earned him the nickname 'Bhalu' in the Academy.

To spar in mock fights during classes was a totally different thing from getting into the ring. Just trying to keep the arms up in a sparring position for three minutes in the ring was a Herculean task for me.

We had to fight three rounds. In the first round of three minutes, Dhillon chased me and I circled around the entire ring, trying to avoid him. It was a cat-and-mouse game where yours truly was the mouse. Despite my best efforts, I finally got cornered. It was a do or die moment. Left with no option, I landed a solid punch on his jaw with all the power I possessed. The bear was not expecting a punch, and it shook him. I was amazed at my punch.

I got bolder, and in the second round, I stood my ground and faced him. The match was now evenly poised. In the last round, it was again a cat-and-mouse game, but this time, Dhillon was the mouse. He parried me, but I managed to land a winning punch. Dhillon fell flat on his back, and the crowd cheered. I was the underdog who had won.

Academics bored us. While most of the cadets were happy doing their outdoor activities, they resented being confined in the classroom for long hours, poring over different subjects.

It was the English class that we found most boring. Shakespeare and Milton didn't interest us, nor did the lopsided grammar. Most of the cadets caught up with the backlog in other subjects, or did their project work while the teacher waxed eloquent about Shelley and Wordsworth. Some wrote letters home, or doodled, or caught forty winks. It was our time to relax. No one took English seriously.

Most of the instructors who took classroom lectures had been in the Academy for long, teaching the same subject year after year, so they were familiar with the attitude of the cadets as well as the lessons.

Mr Raina, our English teacher, was grey with age and

experience. He would start the class by reading a passage from the textbook, which he would continue to read till he came to the name of a place, be it in India or abroad. At that point, he would close the book and start off with his experience in that particular place.

'Once when I was in London ...'

'Last summer, when I was in Darjeeling ...'

'I still carry fond memories of my visit to Spain ...'

'When I was in the US with my son ...'

The only time we paid attention was when he narrated his experiences. We would count the number of places in the textbook that he had told us about. If we wanted to hear about London, it was Lesson Fourteen, for Australia it was Lesson Five, and so on. We learnt more about geography than about English in his classes. I don't know whether he recounted fictitious accounts to hold our attention, or he had really visited all the places he told us about. He didn't look like a globe-trotter but he certainly seemed to know a lot about those places.

In our third term, those who cleared the minimum Hindi language test had to opt for a foreign language. Most opted for Chinese and so did I. Our Chinese teacher was the only lady teacher around. She was a petite beauty, who, to our eyes, looked like a Chinese doll though she was a true-blue Indian. When she read from the book, the cadets stared at her without blinking. Each one of us was in love with her. We all fared badly in the Chinese language, since all of us had paid more attention to the teacher than to our lessons.

FIFTEEN

It was a Sunday morning. 'I'm broke,' declared Maachh. 'I am not going to the city this Sunday.'

It was almost the end of the term, and most of us had run out of the extra cash we had brought from home.

'I think I'll also skip liberty this time,' I seconded Maachh, my debt-ridden conscience goading me.

'In that case, I won't go either,' said Randy.

Bertie was dressing up for the Sunday service at church.

We decided to play cricket. 'You can join us after you've finished with your prayers,' Randy told Bertie.

Hours passed but Bertie didn't turn up. We were almost through with the match. 'The Mass is long over. What's keeping the guy, I wonder. I'll go and find him,' said Maachh.

'We'll come with you,' decided Randy. 'He could have got into some trouble.'

As we pedalled from the Sudan Block towards the 'Hut of Remembrance', we found Bertie's cycle lying on the ground. It was the most isolated area in the campus, with thick vegetation all around, the kind of place described in whodunit novels. On most days, no one passed by. One could easily get murdered in the secluded place, and the body could lie undetected for weeks.

Worried, we began hunting for him.

'Where could the guy be?' said Maachh. 'Do you think someone has kidnapped him?'

'Maybe Bulldog decided to do away with him to protect his daughter's chastity,' joked Randy.

We were cackling at the thought when we heard a rustle in the bushes behind a huge banyan tree. Randy quietly shinnied up the tree while we waited. Once he had perched himself on a comfortable branch, he gestured and we also climbed up.

He pointed down at a clearing near the bushes. Silently, we peered down through the foliage from our perch.

There, seated on the ground were Bertie and his girlfriend. Maachh gasped, and was about to speak when Randy clamped a hand over his mouth. The lovebirds were holding hands and speaking in a hushed tone, unmindful of the hidden company.

Randy nodded, and we came down as quietly as we had gone up, picked up our bikes, and pedalled back to the squadron.

'The scoundrel,' Maachh spluttered. 'No wonder he is not going on liberty. The guy has made such rapid progress and not shared a word about it with us.'

'Wonder how she evaded the Bulldog.'

'Do you think he will kiss her?' Maachh sounded bothered.

'We'll know when he returns,' I consoled him.

'That is, if he tells us anything.'

Bertie was grinning from ear to ear as he returned to the squadron.

'So, what happened at the church? Did Jesus finally smile at you?' asked Maachh, pouncing on Bertie the moment he spotted him.

'He did,' said Bertie. 'And what a smile it was!'

Randy came straight to the point. 'We saw you.'

'Where? How?' It was Bertie's turn to splutter. 'I mean ... when?'

'We saw you sitting with the girl, in the bushes, behind the Hut of Remembrance.'

The guy blushed beetroot red, and got all tongue-tied.

'Well, we are waiting,' Maachh reminded him, using Randy's line.

'Actually, Lizzie and I were just talking about things.'

'Things! What things?'

'Just things!' Bertie had decided not to spill the beans. There was no point in pestering him.

'How did she get away from the Bulldog?' asked Randy.

'The family was supposed to go for lunch at a relative's place in the city after attending the morning service in the church. Lizzie told her parents that she was feeling sick so she wouldn't go for the Mass. Once they had gone, she sneaked out to meet me.'

'But, what were you doing behind the bush?' Maachh's question made us all break into laughter. Coming from him, it sounded most sinister.

'I told you, just talking.'

'Just talking,' Maachh was sceptical. 'For that you don't have to hide behind a bush.'

'Let him be,' commanded Randy, interposing himself between the two morons. They looked ready to take each other on, with their eyes ablaze and nostrils flared.

Bertie was in love. There was just no doubt about it. He stared at the moon as though he had never seen it before, his statements about love were punctuated with deep sighs, and he sang romantic songs under the shower – indisputable symptoms of love sickness. Instead of drawing aircraft in his notebooks, he had begun doodling hearts pierced with broken arrows. Some even had blood dripping from them.

Unfortunately, love and NDA training don't go together. In the Academy, the rule was simple – perform or perish. And Bertie had become a non-performer. Twice he had been thrown off his horse while riding, much to the ustaad's ire. His performance at academics was nose-diving, along with his diving performance at the swimming pool. He had been pretty good at cross-country, but now he ran as though he was carrying his cross on the shoulder. Not just that, he displayed lovely bruises on his face after the last boxing match. That he managed to save his nose was his only achievement.

We were concerned.

'We've got to help the chap,' Randy declared after a particularly bad day.

Bertie had managed to sink lower than the backbenchers, in academics. Even Jassi Kalra, who was a known dud, had overtaken him.

'If he continues like this, he is sure to be relegated,' said Randy.

'But what can we do about his performance? He is in love, and a guy in love will turn into a non-performer,' I philosophized.

'We've got to reason with him.'

Reason we did. At least, Randy tried.

'Look buddy, there is no point in letting your performance slip.'

'It is not intentional,' Bertie got defensive immediately.

'No one is saying it is intentional, but you've got to pay a little more attention to your training.'

Bertie began sulking. Our sermon did not please him.

Randy tried a different approach. 'You like the girl, don't you?'

'Of course I do.'

'How will you face her if you got relegated? Think about it,' reasoned Randy.

It worked. The mention of relegation and his girlfriend in the same breath made a dent in his thick skull.

'I had not thought about it,' he mumbled. 'Lizzie wouldn't look at me if I were relegated.'

'There you are,' I butted in. 'You could lose her because of your bad performance. Wouldn't it be better if you did well and impressed her?'

'And in the same stroke you could prove the Bulldog wrong,' added Randy.

The talk worked. Petrified of losing Lizzie, Bertie began making earnest efforts to perk up his grades in every sphere.

SIXTEEN

It was compulsory to opt for a hobby in our third term, and I opted for sailing. On Sunday mornings, we had to cycle down to the Peacock Bay where the boats were moored. The bay was a part of the huge Khadakvasala Lake. We were allotted small boats, which were called the Cadet Class boats. After a few initial classes, we were released in the lake. Though I could swim reasonably well, the huge expanse of water unnerved me. It was my fascination with sailing that finally nullified my fear. The thrill of sailing in the boats on our own seemed to have a touch of romance that never failed to work on me.

On our third day, a cadet called Ranka and I were assigned a small boat and allowed to take it into the water. The experienced and senior cadets had taken bigger boats like the *Enterprise* and the *CBK*.

We were two inexperienced cadets in a boat, and we felt out of depth. Like a true greenhorn, I carried my notes along in case of emergency. The classroom instructions had made sailing seem so simple. Attending them we had felt confident of handling everything, but now, seated in the small boat, every little problem assumed gigantic proportions. The ustaad gave a small shove, and the boat moved out smoothly into the water. It sailed like a dream, and we were ecstatic. Adrenaline surged through my veins as I stood up like Nelson at the helm of his battleship, with only the binoculars missing.

Trouble began a little later when we tried to manoeuvre, and the boat refused to respond. We moved our buttocks rhythmically, as on a swing, to urge it to move, but to no avail. Ranka tried to put up the sail, but the breeze was too mild to effect any change in the boat's position. There were six other boats in the bay, which merrily went around catching the wind in their sails.

After a lot of sweating, we managed to move the boat out of the bay into the open, and the wind filled the sail. Slowly, we began gaining speed. Thrilled with our success, we goaded it to move further from the base. The little boat floated beautifully into the deep blue water. Panic struck when we realized that we had moved farther than we had anticipated. We pulled at the ropes to change direction, but it wasn't as easy a task as it seemed. I found that the boat was taking us for a ride, instead of the other way round. Desperate, I thumbed through my notebook for a solution. The theoretical lessons had not prepared us for practicals.

As we tugged at the ropes, the boat tilted dangerously.

'Let us move to the other side,' I instructed Ranka. 'It will help in balancing the damn thing.'

The two of us jumped to the other side to steady it. The moment we stood up, the boat capsized, and we fell into the water. It was a disgraceful exhibition of ignorance. I no longer felt like Nelson.

The ustaads deployed as lifeguards continued to patrol the lake in a motorboat. They saw us flapping helplessly in the water, but did not respond. They were giving us a good chance to drown ourselves. The two of us were thoroughly drenched and exhausted, trying to get the boat upright. I felt like a rat trapped in a bucketful of water. When all our efforts failed, we decided to abandon the boat, and began swimming towards the base. At this juncture, the ustaads decided to be kind. One of them took the boat away, while the other took us up in the motorboat.

It was small consolation that my pals hadn't fared too well in their hobby classes either. Maachh had taken trekking as a hobby. It was the most popular hobby apart from riding, since it offered an escape from routine. With his predilection for messing things up, there was not much he could ruin, but he returned with lovely bruises after a couple of falls. Bertie, who had opted for Western music had a natural flair for it. Yet, he managed to snap a few strings of his guitar in the very first week.

For Randy, riding was the thing. He was a natural as far as riding was concerned. The way he handled a horse would have shamed a pro.

It was a cloudless night with a clean dark sky when we escaped into our favourite T-55 tank in front of the Sudan Block for a smoke and some loud thinking. The battle tank-without-the-hatch was a place that inspired our tired brains.

There's something about the hormones at our age that hooks girls on the mind as firmly as stickers to the refrigerator door. Girls were an obsession with most of us at the Academy. Having a girlfriend was considered an achievement. Most of us didn't have one, but everyone boasted of knowing a few girls quite intimately.

'Divulge the truth, dear Bong, do you have a girlfriend?' Bertie asked Maachh.

'Arrey, who will look at a guy like me? I am not Randy.'

'How sad!' Bertie was bent upon making fun of Maachh. 'What about sex?'

I shot him a warning look. He was treading on slippery ground. 'I mean, have any of you ever had sex?'

We threw him a dirty look.

'Okay, guys, no offence meant. Just checking.' He threw up his hands in mock surrender. 'I was just wondering ...,' he hesitated. 'Why don't we go to Budhwar Peth one of these days?'

'Budhwar Peth, where's that?' I asked.

'Oh! Budhwar Peth is the red light area of Poona. Don't tell me you have never heard of it,' Randy mocked.

Honestly, I had never heard of the place. I was horrified that Bertie was even thinking of visiting the red light area. Ever since I had sat through the educational film on Sexually Transmitted Diseases, I had been petrified of sex. Most cadets had avoided all talk of sex for many weeks after the film.

'What are you saying?' I gasped. 'Haven't you seen the film on STD?'

'No, Pessi, I was snoring through it,' teased Bertie. 'Tell me about it.'

'Well, it was about unsafe sex. A prostitute is the most likely transmitter of diseases,' I stuttered.

'Honestly, Pessi, if one were to listen to you, one would never do anything in life.'

Bertie slapped his forehead in exasperation.

'Well guys, what are your thoughts on the subject?' he asked the others.

'Right now, I am not in a mood,' said Randy, feigning indifference.

No one wanted to admit that they were under the spell of the documentary.

'Nor am I,' Maachh circumvented the issue.

The truth was that none of us would have dared to visit such a place. It was one thing to talk about sex, and quite another to experiment with it.

'Typical middle-class approach,' cursed Bertie, but we knew he was as nervous as any of us. His bravado did not fool us.

The discussion ended as abruptly as it had begun. It had

made us feel quite hot under the collar.

Certain things can't be evaded for long, and neither could we stem our curiosity about Budhwar Peth. It was a hot topic of discussion with most third-termers. Almost all senior cadets claimed to have visited the area although no one knew for sure. Usually, an ustaad in plain clothes was posted around the area during Sundays, to catch hold of the errant cadets.

Though we bragged about going to the red light area, none of us dared. We were mortally afraid of catching some terrible disease from the females there. In any case, we were quite content studying our files containing Gandhi's Teachings, for the moment.

Everything other than academics cooled off a bit, as the exams approached. Academics were important if one wanted to come into the limelight, and to wear the badge of a torch holder and attend the commandant's tea. As usual, Maachh prepared small chits to stuff into the hemline of his shorts, while I toiled.

'The time you take to prepare those chits can be gainfully spent studying,' I scolded him.

'Mind your business, Gandhi. Do your bit, and let me do mine.' His logic was warped. 'One should not waste one's grey cells cramming things that can be copied. Did you know that the number of grey cells in our brain are limited and irreplaceable?'

'Tell me, honestly,' I persisted. 'How can you read those miniature letters with the invigilator making the rounds?'

'What do you think I carry my magnifying glass for?' he laughed.

My father had repeatedly warned me not to return home with less than seventy-five per cent in any subject. 'And that is a concession I am making because of your outdoor activities,' he had written in the letter. 'I don't want you to turn out to be a dumb brawny man with no intellectual abilities.'

I couldn't afford to let myself down. I had to prove myself as cerebral as the rest of the family.

Randy and I were the most serious guys in our gang, Bertie was half-serious, and Maachh ... well, he was just a madcap.

'Forget the exams, guys, let us have some fun,' he offered every evening. 'Don't you guys need a break? Why don't we go for a stroll to the Gole Market, just for an hour?'

Watching our incredulous faces, he would latch on to Bertie. 'Bertie boy, you could do with some bird watching. Why don't you come with me?'

Tempted, Bertie would sometimes oblige him. Together they would do the rounds, feast their eyes on some females, and return pleased with their feat.

'Life is an exam, yaar,' Maachh spread the light of his philosophy. 'If we slog for each exam, can you imagine what would happen? We would be slogging our entire life away. Life is too exciting for that.'

Although I agreed with him, I couldn't stop cramming the lessons into my brain. I was tuned to perform. My father's pressure ensured that.

We heaved a sigh of relief when the exams were finally over and the routine became a wee bit relaxed.

'Hey, the movie *Patton* is showing in the city!' shouted Maachh, hurrying towards us one evening. 'Let us go to the city this Sunday.'

Most cadets going to town on liberty had seen the movie and had come back raving about it. The preceding Sunday, some of the cadets had bumped into Ferreira at the theatre. That he had been impressed by the movie was evident from his mannerisms and actions that became rather Patton-like thereafter.

To his credit, the deputy tried to get the movie screened at the NDA for all the cadets to watch. He tried very hard, but without result. The Führer, however, was not a man to give up. He hit upon a novel idea of taking the cadets to the town on bicycles one evening, for the movie. All the cadets lined up, and cycled their way through the city, which was a good fifteen kilometres away. Poona had never witnessed anything like this before. Over a 1000 cadets riding on bikes in proper formation, moved towards the movie hall. The traffic police manning the crossroads were awed by the unending stream of cadets flowing past. Impressed, they allowed us to hog the road, stopping all traffic as we passed.

Our invasion of the town was an event that the Poona-ites had never experienced. Crowds gathered to watch us as we passed, and children waved enthusiastically at us, cheering us on the way. The Academy bus and a truck followed our contingent. Whenever a cadet had a problem such as a flat tyre, or brake failure, the truck would pick up the bike, and the bus would seat the cadet. The attention of the city folks accelerated our progress as we continued pedalling in the afternoon heat.

The entire hall had been booked in advance for the cadets. As soon as we had settled in our seats, Maachh began cribbing. 'What is the point in coming for a movie if there are no females around?'

'Have you come to watch the movie or the females?' asked Randy.

'Both,' Maachh replied. He was irrepressible.

The movie was great. An excited lot of cadets cycled back to the Academy that night. Overnight, Patton became the hero for all the cadets. His famous lines, 'No bastard ever won a war by dying for his country, he won it by making the other bastard die for his country,' began to appear on boards and charts in classrooms and squadrons.

An announcement that a fancy dress competition was to be held a week later at the stadium prodded us into action. A host of ideas began floating around, some good, some bad, and some outright weird. Everyone was being secretive. No one wanted to disclose their get-up till the last moment.

Maachh had a brilliant idea of dressing up as a Goan fisherman. 'You can help me with the get-up,' he told Bertie. 'Of what use is a Goan if he can't be of help?'

'I would if I could. Frankly speaking, I am clueless about the kind of dress they wear.'

'Are you a Goan or not?' Maachh persisted.

'I am a Goan but I am not a fisherman,' Bertie retorted.

After drawing a blank from that quarter, Maachh had another brilliant idea. He wanted to watch the movie *Bobby* in which the heroine's father is a Goan fisherman. To his credit, he managed to do full justice to his guise, ultimately. Bertie participated as a Catholic priest. After all his visits to the church, he couldn't have done otherwise. Randy and I helped them with their dresses.

Some smooth-skinned first-termers, with hairless limbs and faces, dressed up as females. Others dressed up like Rommel, Mountbatten, or Patton. With the Fü hrer acting as the chief judge, there were bets on who would carry the day.

Jaggi Singh, a second-term Sikh, had a flawless complexion, so he dressed up like Helen, the famous dancer, and was a great hit. He danced to the tune of a Hindi film, and performed a cabaret, exposing his satin-smooth thighs, which sent the cadets into raptures. He heaved and sighed, pouted and panted, with great effect. At the end of his performance, Jaggi flung himself into the arms of the deputy who was seated in the front row along with the other officers and their wives. Not to be outdone, the deputy got up and lifted him up in his arms, which sent the cadets hooting and whistling.

Maachh, enthused by the film *Bobby*, danced to the tune of 'Ghey, ghey, ghey re sahiba, pyar mein sauda nahiin',which invited catcalls. His two left feet managed to somehow avoid getting tangled up, but his triangular lungi rode up higher and higher with each step, causing a lot of laughter. Bertie effectively held a mini Mass and the Fü hrer was seen crossing himself playfully.

Although there were many generals, Rommel and Patton

were the favourites. Kalra, inspired by the film that we had just watched, dressed up exactly like Patton in the movie, and started off, 'No bastard ever won a war by dying for his country ...' His speech brought the house down.

Betting was rife amongst the cadets. Everyone was sure that Helen would get the first prize, but the prize went to Patton. Kalra won the first prize, with an overwhelming score.

The Academy, with its wide-open spaces, clean paths, and beautifully landscaped gardens, was a favourite place for film shootings. Bollywood directors flocked to the NDA to shoot specific kinds of scenes like those of riding, sailing, and gliding. As for war films, a few scenes shot at the Academy and the firing ranges seemed mandatory. Film shootings generated a lot of excitement as the cadets flocked to see the actors in action. There was also the excitement of taking part in some shots when they needed to shoot crowds. Sometimes, the directors would select a few smart-looking cadets to do a little more than stand in a crowd.

One Sunday morning, while we were sitting outside our cabins, soaking in the sun, Maachh sauntered up with the exciting news.

'Hey guys, the Bombay chaps have arrived. They are shooting at the stables. Rajesh Khanna will be coming in a few hours for the shoot.'

Rajesh Khanna was a superstar at that time, and a hot favourite of many cadets. We rushed to the stables where the film crew had set up their paraphernalia.

They had already selected some cadets for the shot. Minhas, a handsome fellow, was chosen for an important part. In the scene the cadets led by Minhas were to give a chase to the hero, Rajesh Khanna, on horseback.

We stood on the fringes, watching the cadets sweat for a few hours while they waited for the hero and practised their shot. Minhas looked stunning in his riding gear.

'He looks smarter than Rajesh Khanna,' commented Maachh.

'I bet he will give the hero a huge complex,' agreed Bertie.

It turned out to be a boring affair, and we returned to the squadron after a while. The shooting continued till the light faded. After his brush with acting, Minhas started taking himself a little too seriously, and decided to take his chances with the film industry. He began bragging about his shot and spoke of nothing else but Bollywood for the next few days.

After our mid-term break, there was no news of Minhas. Two days into the term, the guy had still not arrived. His parents were notified about his absence, but they knew nothing about the whereabouts of their son. Worried, the parents contacted all their relatives and friends, but to no avail. Minhas had vanished. Even as the anxious parents were debating whether they should notify the police, the prodigal son returned to the Academy. A few days later, we got to know the whole story. The entire Academy was abuzz with Minhas's tryst with Bollywood.

Our hero had run away to Bombay to try his luck at acting. He went straight to the director who had given him the little role of chasing Rajesh Khanna on horseback, but the man refused to recognize him. Frustrated, Minhas roamed around from studio to studio, trying for a break in the movies. It was only when his money finished, and Bollywood doors were shut on his face, that he returned to the Academy. His parents heaved a sigh of relief and so did his friends at the Academy. As a punishment for his offence, Minhas was relegated and the poor guy never spoke of Bollywood again.

The news from the front was not good. Infiltration on the western border was at a high, and the probability of India going to war with Pakistan had increased. Troop movement was reported, but the news was sketchy. Preparations for the war, and the POP, continued simultaneously. A few officers were quickly posted out of the NDA to border areas, and tension mounted in the Academy.

We were anxious to know all about the conflict.

As expected, war broke out. More and more transistors were smuggled into the squadron through the room attendants. Pakistan Radio was popular with the cadets who wanted to learn the enemy version of the war. According to the Pakistan propaganda machinery, they had captured the airfields of India, and marched right into the mainland. They gave jubilant reports about the number of Indian soldiers killed by their valiant soldiers. All India Radio reciprocated with conflicting reports and counterclaims. The PR machinery in India countered Pakistan's claim, and reeled out stunning figures of casualties suffered by the Pakistani army.

Randy was a worried man. His brother, who was in the army, was posted at the border. He called up home and spoke to his father. The situation, Randy confirmed, despite all claims by Pakistan, was the other way round. India had penetrated deep inside east Pakistan. Confused by the conflicting reports pouring from all quarters, we gave up both the Pakistan Radio and the AIR, and tuned into the BBC.

Saurav Sen's father, who was commanding an artillery regiment, had to move his troops almost overnight from Pathankot to Jammu. His mother, who was a doctor in the army, was also transferred to Jaisalmer at short notice. His sister was in school, and had to be left with an aunt at Delhi. Sen was also very worried. With his family split up like this, he didn't know whom to contact.

A few days into the war, Ferreira came to the squadron and called for Saurav. There was consternation among us, as the deputy led the cadet away in his car. Later, we learnt that Saurav had lost his father in the Pakistan artillery firing on the western front. The mood in the squadron turned sombre.

There was unanimity in the Academy that the Pakistanis needed to be taught a lesson. All of us wanted to take up the gun and teach the enemy a lesson they wouldn't forget in a hurry.

‘India must drop a nuclear bomb over that country,’ announced Maachh, who was very disturbed after hearing the news about Saurav’s father. It was Bong solidarity at its peak. ‘End of all problems, once and for all.’

‘I wish we were given a chance to fight the ***,’ Bertie gnashed his teeth in anger.

‘Our chance will come,’ replied Randy, coolly. ‘Those *** are not going to give up fighting, and this will not be the last war either.’

Ferreira updated us regularly on the progress of the battle during the POP rehearsals, ‘Bang and dig in your feet as if a Pakistani soldier is under your feet,’ he shouted. Patriotism was running high among the cadets, and he used the emotion to goad us on.

His words had a telling effect, and the noise that emerged from the parade ground seemed to rattle the buildings. Drill, after all, is about banging and digging in of the feet. The rehearsals carried on. Although the rehearsal was quite all right, the deputy said that it was bad and called the Academy out in the evenings for practice. This had never happened before. His high standards were the cause of misery for the cadets.

‘You are fortunate to be a part of one of the best military training schools in the world. You have to live up to its reputation and prove your credentials,’ he barked. ‘Nothing short of excellence is acceptable.’

We responded by performing our part in the best possible manner.

The commandant’s parade was even more impressive. After the commandant left, the deputy arrived and dashed all our hopes by saying, ‘It is customary for the VIP to say that the parade is good, but I say it was a ***ing display!’

The final POP, in which the Chief of Army Staff reviewed the parade, was fantastic. After the parade, Ferreira announced that he had never seen a parade as good as ours. It was better than the POP of the West Point in the US, and Sandhurst in the UK. His words made us swell up with pride. The final part of the parade, in which the band played the 'Auld Lang Syne,' and the entire Academy did a slow march, was perhaps the most impressive part of the show.

The sixth-termers marched out from the front under the quarterdeck, and the others from the rear, to the Quarter Master Fort, in a magnificent display, that brought a lump in every spectator's throat. The entire spectacle evoked patriotism in everyone.

The POP marked the end of the term for the first- to the fifth-termers. For the sixth-termers, it was time to bid goodbye to the Academy after a formal tea with the officers.

SEVENTEEN

It was time for some serious professional training, geared to make us feel like true soldiers. Training in weapons was a vital part of our training. The ustaads who taught military subjects like PT, drill, weapon training, swimming, and other necessary skills, were from the army and were the very best in their profession. Their pattern of imparting instruction was standard throughout the army. It was simple, systematic, and logical. It was meant for the dullest of the dullards. While the instructors taught in English, the ustaads imparted lessons in Hindi, and the textbooks on weapon training were in Hindi.

In our first class on '7.62 Self Loading Rifle' we were made to sit in a small squad of ten cadets. A blackboard and a table were placed before us, and written in bold letters across the blackboard, were the words, '7.62 mm Self Loading Rifle'. While the heading was clearly visible to everyone, the text under it was covered with long paper strips. The strips covered the sequence in which the lesson was to be conducted, and as the instructor completed one phase, he removed the paper strip and went on to the next. The sequence went like this:

Introduction
Parts
Functions
Working
Trouble-shooting
Conclusion

On the table lay a SLR Rifle covered with a white bedsheet.

The ustaad arrived, marching smartly, and stood at attention between the board and the table, while we watched intently. With dramatic deliberation, he looked at the board, seeming to study the words written on it. He then carefully lifted the bedsheet covering the rifle, peeped under it cautiously, lifted it by a few millimetres and then covered it up again.

Finally, having finished his inspection, he was ready for the lesson. He drew in a deep breath and asked pompously, 'Cadets, to soche aur bataein, aj ka lesson kya hai (Cadets, think carefully and tell me, what is today's lesson about?).'

We all knew the topic as it was given in the weekly programme, distributed a week in advance. Besides, it was there right in front of us, written in block letters on the blackboard. It was sheer stupidity to ask such a dim-witted question. But we decided to play along. The ustaad paused dramatically near RP and asked: 'Cadet RP Singh, aap bataein (You tell us).'

'Danda (stick),' RP Singh got up and answered with a straight face. Although dying to break into laughter, we managed to maintain a solemn expressions.

'Takreeban theek, baith jayen (Almost correct, sit down).'

Rather pleased with the effort, the ustaad went down the aisle, 'Cadet Nath?'

'Pistol.'

'Takreeban theek, baith jayen.'

It was a premeditated decision that no one would give the

right answer. On his part, the ustaad never declared any answer as wrong. His 'takreeban theek' was supposed to motivate us.

After having asked a few more cadets, the ustaad shrugged and strode back to the table, pretending to be exasperated with our stupidity. His strategy of 'takreeban theek' had not succeeded in eliciting the correct answer.

Then, with a flourish, he removed the bedsheet, and uncovered the rifle lying under it, like a genie unravelling a miracle. 'Aaj ka sabak hai, Self Loading Rifle 7.62 mm. (Today's lesson is Self Loading Rifle 7.62mm).'

Thereafter, like a robot, he began parroting the facts and details, teaching the cadets as though he was instructing a class of mentally challenged kids. With the kind of answers he had received to the simple queries, it was not his fault if he took us to be nitwits.

The questions asked by the ustaads were invariably funny. Initially, we would laugh until we cried, but gradually, we got used to the questions and remained stone-faced like the ustaads themselves, when someone gave an equally funny answer.

Some of the question-answer sessions went like this:

'Three-men trench mein kitne log fit aaten hain (How many men can fit into a three-men trench)?' the ustaad would ask.

We would answer, 'Do (two), chaar (four), or panch (five).'

The ustaad would not get angry because he thought we were buffoons. Finally, he would announce, 'takreeban theek,' and in a self-important manner, give out the correct answer. 'Cadets, dhyan dein. Three-men trench mein teen log fit aaten hain (Cadets, listen carefully. Three men can fit into a three-men trench).'

The terminology used by the ustaads was a real howler. Indication of reference points was a genuine example of 'humour in uniform'. It went something like this:

'Samney dekh, 100 metres, ek chota pond, naam: Hema

Malini (Look to your front, 100 metres, a small pond, name: Hema Malini).'

No one ever questioned the logic of the names given to the reference points. For some mysterious reasons, a round tree was called Kabutar. Still more mysterious was the significance of naming a tall mountain Simi, after the actress. The most popular reference point was a pair of mountain tips called Begum Para's tits. The references never failed to draw a spate of chuckles from the cadets.

At times, the reference points were so numerous that names had to be borrowed from Hollywood. Marilyn Monroe was a hot favourite.

Workshop classes were conducted in the Science Block. It was the only place where one got an opportunity to exercise one's imagination. We were taught a whole lot of things like the blacksmith's trade, tinning, foundry work, carpentry, working on lathe machines ... things we would never get to learn anywhere else.

These classes were conducted normally after double outdoor exercise and breakfast, not really the best time for such activities. With their bellies full of a sumptuous breakfast, most of the cadets looked forward to a good nap instead. The workshop with its huge area and umpteen nooks and corners was ideally suited for the much-desired snooze. A few keen cadets would keep the instructors busy, while characters like Maachh and Bertie stole into one of the nooks to grab a refreshing siesta. Most of the cadets marked their attendance and slunk off, either to the library or to their rooms.

The workshop was a great place to extract revenge. All one had to do was spoil the other one's job. Of course, there were some cadets who were quite serious about the workshop, and spent their time creating and crafting exclusive items quite sincerely. Maachh, who was never interested in anything laborious, loitered around looking for cadets who had irritated him in some manner.

Once he drilled a large hole in the box Rocky was making. It was his act of revenge against the cadet for not lending him a fag during the break.

News travelled to Ferreira that quite a few cadets frequently skipped their classes by hiding in the library. The Fü hrer, infuriated by the intelligence, decided to raid the library. His umpteen attempts at catching the cadets red-handed failed to yield a satisfactory result. The smarter ones always managed to elude him, the cadets pitting their wits against those of the Fü hrer. Ultimately, things reached such a stage that it became a challenge for the deputy to trap at least a couple of offenders, to salvage his reputation of being a stern disciplinarian.

After having tried all kinds of tricks, the Fü hrer devised a novel technique to catch the offenders. He came up to the first floor, stamping his foot, and creating a din near the library door, as if he was entering the library. The moment they heard him arriving, the cadets inside tried to escape by jumping through the library windows. Changing his tracks, the deputy quickly ran down the stairs to the cycle stand, and hid himself. His manoeuvre resulted in netting a few fellows who had jumped off the first floor. As the news of his modus operandi spread through the Academy, even the veteran sixth-termers ran shy of hiding in the library to skip classes.

At the time, it was the height of cricket fever, and every cadet wanted to keep himself updated by listening to the commentary on the radio. The library was the favourite haunt of the cadets during such times too. One could easily lose oneself behind the racks of books and listen to the commentary, undisturbed by the instructors. It was also the time when the Fü hrer decided to trap the offenders and set an example by doling out severe punishments to them.

One day, while passing the library, Ferreira heard a transistor playing inside. He cocked his ears and listened; sure enough someone was listening to the cricket commentary. Although he managed to sneak in quietly, the cadet turned out a tad quicker, and by the time the deputy entered, silence reigned in the library. Not a person to give up easily, Ferreira rounded all the cadets present inside the library and barked, 'Out with the transistor, or I will punish the whole lot of you.'

He raved and ranted and hunted everywhere for the transistor set, but to no avail. After a fruitless search of an hour, he finally gave up.

Tired, he announced, 'Gentlemen, I give up. I would like to shake hands with the guy who has beaten me in the battle of wits. Hats off to him!'

But the cadets were no fools. They didn't trust the Fü hrer. In front of almost sixty cadets that he had rounded up, the deputy declared, 'I promise that no action will be taken against the culprit. It is a gentleman's word. I just want to know where the wretched transistor has been hidden.'

When a guy as senior as the deputy promises and gives a gentleman's word, he can no longer be ignored. Rana, a fourth-term cadet, quietly walked out of the library, and went to the ground floor. Walking up to the huge bougainvillea tree that bloomed just under the library window, he brought out a satchel in which the transistor was neatly wrapped. He had hurled it from the first floor window when he saw the deputy entering the library. Tension mounted amongst the cadets in the library as they waited for the deputy's reaction with bated breath. And then Ferreira began to clap. After waiting for a tense minute, the entire lot joined him in clapping. The ovation was meant as an appreciation for Rana's quick thinking.

After the applause died down, the deputy spoke up. 'Boy,' he thundered, 'now you have had it.'

Without batting an eyelid Rana reminded him, 'Sir, you are a gentleman.'

The meaning was clear. A gentleman did not break his word.

Sixty pairs of eyes looked unblinkingly at the Führer, their silent stares announcing their solidarity. Defeated, Ferreira shook hands with Rana and walked out without a word. The cheer that went up as he departed was thunderous.

EIGHTEEN

The end of the term was comparatively free. The tests had finished, and we were more relaxed. To celebrate the relaxed flow of life, a fancy dress competition was planned for the first weekend. Since the first fancy dress had been a super hit, the attendance for this one was supposed to go up by several notches.

As usual, the fancy dress competition generated a lot of enthusiasm in the Academy. It was an event that brought in the entire lot of cadets both as participants and audience.

Popular events generally caused hierarchical problems, since every individual of some importance wanted to hog the limelight. And assertion of importance could find no better means than being invited as the chief guest. For the first fancy dress, the deputy had been the chief guest. When the commandant heard about the thumping success of the event, he also wanted to attend the show. Naturally, then, he would attend it as the chief guest. The family members of the officers and the civilian instructors were also supposed to attend the show.

Rehearsals were on in earnest. As it turned out, the cadets

were not an imaginative lot. It was a repetition of the same old ideas and the same old stunts. The young sardars let their hair down and dressed up as popular actresses, sadhus or hippies, while the others decked up as Rommel, Montgomery, Hitler and Patton, as earlier. It went without saying that those who dressed up as actresses preferred to perform a cabaret, and dance to a Hindi number, while the war heroes delivered famous speeches.

On the final day, it was Manjeet Singh, a cute first-term sardar, dressed up as Zeenat Aman, who carried the day. He swayed and gyrated like the film star, to a hit number, sending the cadets into raptures. His perfect imitation of the star got him the first prize and the title of 'Academy Chick' was conferred upon him.

It was Navy Ball time in Bombay and the Fü hrer, being from the navy, seemed to miss the much-hyped Navy Ball. Inspired, he hit upon the brilliant idea of arranging a jam session for the cadets.

The excitement his idea generated was unprecedented. A jam session had never happened in the Academy. And when Ferreira announced that the cadets could bring their girlfriends from town and entertain them in the mess, the cadets went berserk. For once, his excesses were forgotten as well as forgiven.

'Man, the deputy is a great guy,' announced Maachh. 'Imagine allowing the cadets to dance with girls!'

He was thrilled at the prospect of meeting some girls, as was every other cadet.

'God bless the Fü hrer for his great ideas,' seconded Bertie, excited that he could now dance with Lizzie without any fear. With the deputy sanctioning the event, even her parents would not object.

The problem most cadets faced was that they didn't have girlfriends. A dance party could not happen without dance partners, it was as simple as that. So the deputy invited the girls who were studying medicine at the Armed Forces Medical College.

When my cousin, a local from Poona, heard that guests were being invited for the party, he decided to attend the party.

'I can bring a few girls along,' he told me over the phone. 'My classmates will be glad to attend the event.'

The news thrilled my girl-starved friends.

On the appointed day my cousin turned up with his friends, three boys and five girls, all from the same college. There was still some time before the jam session began, so I showed them around the Academy, after which we landed up in the squadron anteroom.

The cadets were dressed in their best togs to go to the mess for the jam session. The air was thick with the smell of cologne and aftershave lotions.

As soon as I entered the anteroom with my friends, the cadets noticed the five girls in our group. Soon, the entire squadron trickled in into the anteroom. I introduced everyone and the ice was broken. Someone put the music on, and the room vibrated with chatter. The atmosphere was right for a jam session right there in the anteroom.

Initially, the music was soft, and then, someone asked one of the girls to dance. Thereafter, there was no stopping the cadets. The floor was full of gyrating bodies, and the music steadily got louder. A few cadets who had brought their girlfriends joined in, and everyone let their hair down. With the music at its peak, it overpowered the one originating from the mess. The crowd grew in proportion to the decibels.

The mess wore a deserted look. Although the music was playing, and all arrangements had been made, barely a few cadets loitered around the place. A few seniors who had gone to the mess, did not find company, and hearing the loud music in the G squadron, they made a beeline towards the anteroom.

The lights were dimmed, the music turned up, and the floor filled up with dancing pairs. Oblivious of the time and the happenings around, our party continued well past the allotted time of 6.00 p.m.. Bertie, with his skill in dancing, was much in demand and flirted with finesse.

On the other hand, Maachh, with his two left feet, found not a single girl who was willing to risk her toes by dancing with him. Not to be disheartened, the poor chap continued to do his stumbling act on one side of the hall. It was Randy, tall and debonair, who attracted girls by the drove. Too shy to ask any of the girls for a dance, Natty was happy watching them from a distance.

Lavish snacks had been laid out for the party at the mess. Since there was no arrangement for eats in the squadron, the cadets had their fill of snacks at the mess, and returned to the squadron to enjoy themselves. Some even dared to carry liberal amounts of snacks back to the squadron. Despite the arrangements at the mess, there was a bigger crowd at the squadron.

Wondering where all the cadets had disappeared, the deputy decided to investigate. As he crossed the G squadron, he heard loud music blaring from it. The moment his car came to a screeching halt in front of the squadron, all the cadets vanished from the anteroom. The music ceased, and all that remained were ten girls and their civilian escorts. Pin-drop silence greeted the Führer as he entered the anteroom.

'What happened to the music? Who put it off?' he asked the girls. 'Come on, play some music. Let's dance.' Music and cheer filled the hall once again, and the dancing resumed. Ferreira joined in the revelry. The cadets who were peeping from the windows were taken aback to see the Führer dancing with abandon. Cautiously, they trickled back, relieved that the deputy was not on warpath.

After about fifteen minutes, Ferreira switched off the music and announced, 'The party is over, gentlemen, now off to work.' And he drove off.

There was nothing more to be done, so we dispersed reluctantly. It was great while it lasted.

The much-awaited cricket test series between India and West Indies had begun, and listening to the commentary was a big craze, especially on the sly since the cadets were not allowed to possess transistors. Many sixth-termers would skip their classes to listen to the commentary. They would get their cabins locked from outside by some junior or civilian orderlies, and listen to the commentary undisturbed.

The civilian orderlies continued to work in the squadrons much after the cadets left for their classes. They would collect the leather and canvas items from the allotted rooms, take them to a corner, and polish them. Some cadets left the cabin keys with the orderlies for them to do up the rooms.

One fine afternoon, Ferreira was on the prowl. No deputy had ever strolled the vacant squadrons during the parade hours, but the Fü hrer didn't abide by any rules other than those set by him. Although he had banned transistors from the squadron, he carried his set with him wherever he went, to keep abreast with the latest score.

As Ferreira passed through the corridor on the top floor, Dey, a sixth-termer who was locked up in his room heard the commentary emanating from Ferreira's transistor. Presuming it to be another sixth-termer, Dey shouted 'Kya score hai, yaar (What is the score, buddy)?'

Ferreira was taken aback.

'Come out you scoundrel, I will tell you the score,' roared the Fü hrer banging on the Dey's cabin door.

The dialogue that ensued after Dey emerged from his room is not known; in all probability, it was a monologue. All we got to know was that the poor man got relegated. Cadets were normally relegated for academics, outdoor performance, or on medical grounds. But sometimes, they also got relegated due to their misconduct. In the Academy, as in other facets of life, it did not matter if you broke the rules, but it was important not to get caught.

While Dey got caught, Moga missed getting caught by a whisker. He was already a brigadier (having been relegated for a term), and getting caught would have made him a general.

It so happened that Moga was also listening to the transistor at the very moment when Ferreira was relegating Dey.

Hari, the civilian orderly, had accumulated the shoes to polish, and left them in a corner of the corridor before going down for a cup of tea. Dressed in his vest and shorts, Moga was standing near the heap of shoes with his transistor. On hearing the Fü hrer's steps, he quickly hid the transistor, sat down near the shoes, and began polishing them. 'Ram, Ram, sahib (Good morning, sir),' he greeted the deputy as he passed by. For good measure, the cheeky chap also offered to polish the Fü hrer's shoes. 'Joota chamka doon, sahib (Shall I polish your shoes, sir)?'

The deputy looked down at his shoes and realized that they could do with a shine. He put his foot forward for the shoes to be polished. Moga had a tough time camouflaging his grin while he polished them

That day Moga missed becoming a general, but he definitely achieved the distinction of having hoodwinked the Fü hrer.

NINETEEN

The word that Gary, Girish Chopra, had visited Budhwar Peth was doing the rounds of the squadron. It was considered a great feat. The film on STD (Sexually Transmitted Diseases), shown to us in the first term, had its effect for a long time and managed to keep us away from the red light area. But as time went by, the lessons were forgotten, and the cadets became more adventurous. Although everyone would have liked to experience the delights of Budhwar Peth, not many had the guts to visit the place.

Gary enjoyed bragging. When he told us of his visit to the restricted zone, we took it with a pinch of salt.

'He is just fooling around,' said Randy. 'He wouldn't dare to step anywhere close to it.'

But the rumours of his exploits continued. So we decided to confront him. In the Academy, a guy who had managed such exploits was in great demand. Everyone wanted to hear the story from the horse's mouth.

We flocked to his room to glean the details from him, but he circumvented our questions and changed the topic.

We tried to reach the truth several times, and failed.

One night, he finally decided to bare his heart. As usual, we had gathered in his room after dinner.

'Come on, you moron,' needled Bertie. 'Share the experience with us guys.'

'It was heavenly, yaar,' said Gary closing his eyes and throwing his hands up as if he had experienced nirvana. 'I didn't feel like coming back,' he continued. 'You can't imagine the size of her ***.'

Goggle-eyed, Randy, Maachh and I prodded him for more, while Bertie stared sceptically at him.

'What was her name?'

'What did she look like?'

'How old was she?'

'What was the room like?'

'What exactly did you do?'

'Was she clean?'

'How much did you pay?'

'How long did you stay?'

We flooded him with hundreds of questions.

'Hold it, guys,' he said. 'Let me tell you the way it was.'

He then went on to describe the entire experience in great detail.

Gary's description went exactly the way I had seen in a Hindi movie, the previous weekend. There were kinks in his narration. I did not want to throw a spanner into his imagination, so I let him continue. He spun yards of yarn, and finally got entangled in them.

'Buddy, did you go to see a movie last weekend?' I asked, at the end of his narrative.

The question surprised him, and he creased his brows thoughtfully, wondering where all this was leading to.

'Yes, I did,' he admitted.

'And was that movie called *Ek Nazar*?'

'Yes, it was.'

'There you are, guys. Gary is narrating the story of that movie,' I told the gang. 'He hasn't stepped anywhere near Budhwar Peth.'

Gary never boasted about his visit again. But the bragging didn't end with him; there were many others in the ring. Next weekend, while on their way to the town, Tushar and Natty showed us the condoms they were carrying in their pockets. The same evening at dinner, after their return from the outing, Tushar sat by my side. Over a bowlful of steaming chicken soup, his soul screaming to be purged, he confessed that they had not stepped anywhere near Budhwar Peth.

'Don't tell the others,' he hesitated. 'When we set out from the Academy, Natty and I were absolutely confident about making a visit to the place, but once we reached the city, we chickened out,' he said, unburdening his heart.

Unaware that Tushar had already spilled the beans, Natty carried on the charade. After dinner, over a few fags inside the battle tank, Natty provided vivid details about the imaginary tryst they had with females in the forbidden lanes of Budhwar Peth.

'The experience is impossible to describe,' he began. He closed his eyes, as though he was traipsing down the memory lane. 'There are certain things in life that need to be experienced. They can't be expressed.'

'But, you can certainly describe the procedure,' insisted Maachh.

We were eager to hear his spiel.

'Well, there was this girl – she had the perfect figure – the 36-24-36 kind, and a mesmerizing smile. When I approached her, she smiled, and led me to her room ...'

He paused for effect and we held our breath.

'What did she wear, or not wear?' asked Bertie.

'She was wearing a short, very short skirt with red polka-dots, and a blouse which was knotted at the waist and had a deep plunging neckline.'

His description fitted the scene from a Hollywood film *Irma La Douce* we had recently watched in the city. Randy winked at me and I winked back. We were enjoying the narration.

'And what was the room like?'

'It was like any other room.'

'Oh, skip the room, what you did in it is the issue,' said Maachh. He was getting impatient. He was totally involved in the story.

Natty cleared his throat thoughtfully and continued. 'I was nervous because it was my first time, but she was experienced so she guided me all the way.'

'Arrey yaar, you are a total sadist,' yelled Maachh. 'Why don't you tell us the details?'

His allegation upset Natty. 'Look, I am telling you everything as best as I can. I can't help it if you are not satisfied. For more explicit details, you will have to go there yourself,' he said, ending his yarn. Poor chap, it was a test of his imagination and he had already milked it dry.

'You are in the wrong profession,' remarked Randy, at the end of the narrative. 'You have just missed your vocation,' Bertie and I whispered conspiratorially.

Natty took offence. 'What do you mean by that?' He directed a murderous scowl at Randy.

'Just that you would have made a good name for yourself if you had gone to Bombay.'

Before the implication of the statement could sink in, and Natty could react to it, Randy walked away. No one ever asked Natty about his experience again.

While the most of us were spent time dreaming of Budhwar

Peth and its offerings, it was two gutsy guys from our term, Sood and Pawar, who became overnight heroes.

Each squadron had four officers who were posted on night duty by turns. One night, Flight Lieutenant Tiwari was on duty. The officer had left his motorcycle in the parking lot while he was sleeping in the Fox squadron. No officer ever locked his vehicle inside the campus. Neither did Tiwari.

Sood and Pawar, two fifth-termers, were in a mood to taste the nightlife of the city. They had managed to lay their hands on the keys of a Jawa motorcyle, which, in those days, was common for all Jawas. They quietly pushed Tiwari's bike for a distance, and when they were sure that no one could hear them, they started it with a kick and took off.

At about 1.00 in the night, a sudden announcement ordering an immediate fall-in resounded through our squadron. Rubbing our eyes, and clad in our robes, we rushed down the stairs and gathered in the squadron parade ground.

There was a commotion as more officers arrived and conferred amongst themselves. It seemed to be a serious matter. 'Where is the fire?' whispered Randy.

'Must be in the deputy's pants,' retorted Bertie cheekily.

'Shucks, man!' cursed Maachh. 'After a tiring day, they don't even allow one to grab the eight-hour beauty sleep at night.'

The counting of cadets revealed Sood and Pawar to be missing. Where could they be?

The suspense continued for about an hour. Like zombies we continued to stand in the parade ground, cursing all involved.

At around 3.00 in the morning, Sood and Pawar were brought back to the squadron in a police van, and we were finally allowed to go back to sleep.

It was only the next morning that we got to know of the details. Call it a premonition or whatever, Flight Lieutenant Tiwari had suddenly woken up. He peeped out of his window, and found his bike missing. He immediately rang up the city police and reported that his bike had been stolen.

The police swung into action right away, and rounded up Sood and Pawar, who had just finished their business at Budhwar Peth.

The two were brought before the deputy commandant, the next morning. The seriousness of their offence required grave consideration, so the parents were summoned.

Pawar's father was a colonel in the artillery, while Sood belonged to a business family. After serious deliberation, Pawar was relegated for a term, while Sood, who already had a few offences to his discredit, was thrown out of the Academy.

For a while after the incident, no cadet dreamt of Budhwar Peth and its inhabitants – at least not for a long while.

Bertie's romance had reached its peak. Almost every other day, he stole to the Gole Market and rang up Bulldog's residence. If either of Lizzie's parents picked up the phone, Bertie quickly hung up. But if Lizzie came on the line, his day would turn brighter. They fixed up meetings at the tennis court or the Gole Market. His visits to the church did not stop either. He was floating on cloud nine.

One Sunday, after his church appointment, he came back morose.

'What ails you, my friend?' asked Randy.

'He looks like a monkey that has swallowed a cobra, and doesn't know whether to gobble it down or spit it out.' Maachh tried hard to describe Bertie's expression with an utterly ridiculous simile.

'Shut up,' retorted our pal-in-pain.

'Do you have a toothache, buddy?' asked the irrepressible Bong.

'Will you please keep this guy away from me?' requested Bertie. We complied with his wish and silenced the Fish.

'Okay, spill,' ordered Randy. When Randy took on that tone, no one defied him.

'It is Lizzie,' began Bertie. As if we didn't know it. 'She has found someone else.'

'What?' The three of us suffered synchronized shocks.

'What makes you think she has abandoned you for someone else?' I asked.

'For the past few days she hadn't stopped talking about the distant cousin who was coming to visit them. He is a moneyed chap settled in the USA. Then she told me that he had brought a whole lot of gifts for her. Today, at the church she hung on to him like a bougainvillea creeper, and failed to recognize me when I smiled at her.'

'Maybe she wanted to pull wool over the cousin's eyes,' suggested Maachh.

'It is over, I know it. It was there in her eyes. She has even begun speaking in a foreign accent to please the guy.'

'That doesn't mean that she has forsaken you. Maybe she's just trying to impress him.' We tried to console the guy.

'Why should she do that if she is not interested in him?'

'Because she wants more gifts... foreign perfumes, for instance. Girls do a lot of things for such stupid material things. I know it,' Maachh interposed.

'Don't be stupid,' scolded Randy.

Turning to Bertie he asked, 'Did you have a tiff with her?'

'No, I never disagree with her.'

'Then don't worry. All this means nothing.'

'That is not all,' he wailed. 'When I caught up with her near the car park, she froze me with a cold look and hissed dangerously. "Don't follow me", she ordered.'

'Bertie boy, don't give up hope. She will come around,' Randy soothed.

She never did. Lizzie opted for Mr Moneybags over our Goan

boy. Some things never change... girls' preference for well-heeled chaps, for instance. Bertie was heartbroken. He moved around the squadron like a ghost from another century. The world seemed to have collapsed around his ears although we did our best to distract our pal. Randy's prescription was, 'Give it time, buddy, no girl is worth so much trouble.'

In a way, Lizzie's exit from his life proved to be a boon for Bertie. The failed romance continued to depress him for some time but within a few months, he recovered from the heartbreak and directed all his energies into the training. We heaved a sigh of relief at the fast recovery.

We were now in our fifth term. The fun times were over; it was time to perform. From the fifth term, our training groups for the army, navy and air force got segregated. The office holders for the sixth term were also to be decided at the end of fifth term. The cadets who had been performing well were in the race for the honours. The posts of SCC (squadron cadet captain), three DCCs (divisional cadet captains), CSM and the CQMS were the most coveted ones.

Randy, Bertie, and I, were in the fray, and so was Ravi. We knew that none of us would be appointed as a CSM because that office was reserved for the most ruthless chap, and Ravi was the most befitting chap for the appointment. He had already begun to behave like one. Although he was not good at academics, he was good at outdoor activities. He knew that if he did well at outdoors, he would certainly be the CSM, so he practised hurdles running over easy chairs in the corridor, by night. In a way, his practice paid off as, later, he went on to become the NDA record holder for the 400-m low hurdles.

Natty and Maachh knew very well that they were low down in the merit list, and out of the race, so they continued to have good time. 'Life is too short to spend slogging,' was their motto.

Life became a lot more serious – especially for the competitive lot. Randy was good both at games and academics, and way ahead of the pack. Although Bertie was a late starter, having turned serious after his romance fizzled out, he did well in the fifth term. His grades improved appreciably after his heartbreak and our pep talk. I had been good at academics throughout the training. The only weak points were the outdoors activities and I had to work hard on these to catch up with the others.

We envied guys like Maachh and Natty, who continued to enjoy themselves. They were least interested in grades, and just wanted to pass out of the Academy without being relegated. Maachh knew his limitations, and didn't harbour any lofty ambitions. Appointments mattered for those who were from a fauji (army) background, as there was pressure on them from the home front. For Randy, it mattered most. His entire khandaan (family) was in the army, and they knew the ins and outs of the services.

'You guys are lucky,' he said. 'I have to bag an appointment. The old man will not accept any excuses.'

So, the poor guy laboured on all fronts.

At the end of our fifth term, when the results were announced and the appointments declared, Randy had bagged the prestigious appointment of SCC. Bertie, Haldar, and I, were designated as DCCs; and Ravi, the toughie, became the CSM, as expected. For Bertie and me it was a pleasant surprise.

Lucky Maachh was now the only odd man out in our group who could continue to lead an irresponsible life. With the appointment came the responsibilities, and Randy, Bertie, and I, had the duty of running the squadron.

'Our carefree life has come to an end,' Randy announced with regret, the day after we were awarded the stripes. 'From now on, life is going to be tough.' Didn't we know it!

As the countdown began for the POP, the sixth-termers relinquished their charge, and we found ourselves in the thick of all the action. There were times when our conscience was in a dilemma, and we had to choose duty over friendship. With both Maachh and Natty in a wayward mood, it was a difficult option to exercise.

One day, Natty was caught smoking by Sharma, a sixth-termer. The two had gone through a spat a while back, and were looking for opportunities to score over each other. Sharma immediately reported the matter to the CSM. The CSM, in turn, made Natty go through the indignities of punishments. This was too much of an insult for the fifth-termers. We were almost at the end of our fifth term, and such punishments were generally not warranted. For this occasion, we chose camaraderie over responsibility.

'That guy needs to be sorted out,' stated Bertie. 'It was absolutely underhand of Sharma to sneak.'

'No one squeals on our gang and gets away,' seconded Maachh.

A collective decision was taken. Sharma was to be taught a lesson he wouldn't forget in a hurry.

The opportunity arrived on a Saturday, a movie day, when we got to know that Sharma was not going for the movie. Most of the cadets were away at the theatre. The three of us pretended we were going for the movie, and created a lot of din while moving out of the squadron. We loitered around for a while, and sneaked back after the movie had started. The squadron was almost deserted.

Sharma was having a bath, singing at the top of his voice. We got hold of a blanket each, and crept towards the bathroom. As soon as he emerged from the bathroom, we flung the blankets on him, and began raining blows on his back. Two juniors, who saw us, also joined in. Juniors were always looking for a chance to get their hands on seniors.

When we had taken the wind out of him, we dragged him to the toilet, submerged his head into the commode, and flushed his face. Then we blindfolded him, tied his hands behind his back, dumped him in the bathroom, and vanished.

At dinner-time, after the movie, Sharma arrived adorned with bruises in a wide range of black-and-blue. Bertie asked him innocently, 'What happened, sir?'

'I slipped in the bathroom,' was all the poor chap could say.

Then came a time when everyone was down with high fever. I can't say how high the temperature was, but my guess is that it was close to 105 degrees and still rising. Every six months we suffered from the malady of examination fever, and it could go as high as 110 degrees in case of the chaps who had napped during the study periods. Maachh was, of course, one such person. Never known for his academic brilliance, he developed bouts of high fever during the term-end exams. This time was no different.

I caught him making chits on toilet paper, the night before the chemistry exam. Foxed at his love for the toilet roll, I asked, 'Why are you writing on toilet paper?'

He shook his head irritably and told me to get lost.

The next morning, as we began answering the chemistry paper, I stole a look at him. The chap extricated the little bits of toilet paper from his pencil box and cast furtive looks all around. The invigilator was standing at the other end of the hall. Maachh got busy copying from the little pieces of toilet paper on which he had painstakingly written down the formulae.

It so happened that the chemistry laboratory assistant, an old foe of Maachh was on invigilation duty. As he paced around the room, he spotted our dear friend copying from the chits.

'Stop! You there!' the 'lab ass' screamed, bounding towards Maachh's desk. 'Raise your hands.'

For a moment Maachh looked cornered. The next minute he had swallowed the toilet paper chits. We stopped writing and waited for the fireworks. It turned out to be a damp squib. Maachh was too smart to be caught.

A thorough search of his person revealed no chits, much to the frustration of the lab ass. 'I saw you cheating,' he fumed, but failed to find any evidence.

Maachh, however, swore vengeance on the poor fellow. 'He humiliated me in front of the whole class,' he raged.

'But you were cheating,' I sermonized.

'He couldn't find any chits on me.' Maachh's logic was crazy.

'You swallowed them!' I said accusingly.

'So? Can you imagine how difficult it is to swallow toilet paper? It is hard work, I tell you.'

His chance to settle scores with the lab ass came during the chemistry practicals.

'I am going to throw some *aqua regia* on that chap's face,' Maachh said, gnashing his teeth viciously. The only thing he had learnt was that aqua regia was the strongest acid that was capable of dissolving almost all metals, including gold.

He proceeded to create the reagent. 'One part concentrated hydrochloric acid and three parts concentrated nitric acid,' intoned Maachh as he mixed the acids in a glass beaker. His face took on a wicked look as he stared at the resultant mixture.

Spying the lab assistant's watch on the table, Maachh stole up to it and pushed it down his pocket. With a victorious smile he plonked it into the reagent and added some more acid for effect. God knows what he had added because a moment later, there was a loud bang and deadly fumes began emanating from the beaker. Dropping the beaker, Maachh quickly scampered to the other side of the laboratory and busied himself with the salt analysis test before the lab ass could reach the accident spot.

'Who did this?' he shouted, scanning our faces for evidence.

There was no reply. From the other end of the room, I caught the feigned seriousness on Maachh's face. He was studying the ongoing reaction in a test tube as though his life depended on it.

'Who put my watch into the acid?' the lab ass repeated. 'It is a serious offence. Come clean or I will report the matter,' he threatened us.

No one replied. We knew he wouldn't report the matter because he would have to answer for his carelessness, too.

Despite all efforts, the poor assistant could never discover the identity of the culprit who had dropped his watch in the acid.

The exams were also a time for settling old scores and fuelled a lot of competitive energy in everyone. Bertie had an ongoing feud with Balakrishnan, the brains in our batch. Bala, a studious, bespectacled chap, spent much of his time poring over books, either in his room or in the library.

'I hate the guts of that guy,' he announced. 'Why should he be the one to walk away with all the torches each year? I have a strong desire to wipe that smug smile off his mug.'

'Look, Bertie, he slogs through the year while you have a ball. Naturally, he walks away with the prizes.'

'I won't allow the specky to do so this year.'

'And how will you do that?' asked Maachh who was always looking for some action.

The next morning was the mathematics exam and Bala was a whiz kid in the subject.

'I have a plan,' winked Bertie. 'All you guys have to do is to support me.'

The rules of camaraderie dictated that we support a pal, whatever the consequences.

That evening Bertie walked into Bala's room. As expected, the chap was bent over his books, solving complex mathematical problems.

'I say, Specky, don't you ever relax? Your eyes are popping out of their sockets and god, they are as red as tomatoes. There must be something wrong with them.'

On that cue, the three of us, Randy, Maachh, and I, walked in and began commenting on the state of Bala's eyes. 'What happened to your eyes?' shouted Maachh, concern written on his face.

'Have you seen the doc? My dear Specky, I've heard that conjunctivitis is in the air,' Randy added.

'Getting the red-eye at this juncture would be awful. How will you appear for the rest of your papers?' This was the best I could do.

In about ten minutes we had psyched the guy to such an extent that he began to believe that something was terribly wrong with his eyes.

'Do you chaps think that I should go to the MI room?' he asked, worried.

'Look Specky, I happen to have some eye-drops in my room. My mom had given them to me. If you want I can lend the bottle to you,' said Bertie.

I threw him a questioning look.

'Thanks a lot, Bertie. Will you get it for me?'

The scoundrel took off on the double and returned with a bottle. 'Shall I put a few drops in your eyes?'

Without waiting for a reply, Bertie proceeded to put a few drops in Bala's eyes. 'Now just lie down and relax. Keep your eyes closed for ten minutes. You will be all right, don't worry.'

My conscience began to bother me as we walked out of Bala's room.

'Bertie, what was there in that bottle?' I asked. 'The poor chap will not go blind, I hope.'

'Don't worry, Pessi. It is some stuff called atropine, which eye specialists use for dilating the pupils when they want to check the eyes. I stole the bottle from the MI room. The chap won't be able to read. He will see everything magnified many times over, that's all.'

'You shouldn't have done it.' I ended lamely while the rest of the gang burst out laughing at the thought of Bala struggling to focus his pupils.

The next morning, Bala was there, his eyes really red with rage.

'What did you put in my eyes?' he demanded, standing solidly in Bertie's path.

'Did I put something in your eyes? Are you dreaming, dear chap? Why should I put anything in your eyes?' laughed our buddy.

'It is not a joke, you filthy ***! I couldn't read a thing after you put those drops. I still can't see properly.'

'Hope you can read the examination paper,' drawled Bertie.

'Don't worry about that,' retorted Specky.

I felt sorry for the guy.

When the results were declared, things turned out just as they had always done. Bala stood heads taller than all of us. He had scored the maximum in all subjects, maths included. Specky had the last laugh. He walked away with all the academic prizes again that year.

It was time to rejoice. We were going home for the term-end break and we would be the senior-most when we returned.

TWENTY

The break seemed too long as I filled my days at home with friends and family. The fact was that the long absence from home had created a distance between me and my childhood friends. I didn't identify with them any more. Friends now meant the ones I had at the Academy.

I was now six feet tall, athletic in build, intelligent, disciplined, a team player and an all-rounder. There was not a guy in the past generations of our family who had been equally good at swimming, polo, riding, boxing, cross-country, shooting, sailing and what not. I knew a smattering of French and Chinese besides the four languages I had known earlier, which made me a kind of linguist in the family. Relatives paused to admire my muscular physique and upright bearing.

'Your son has single-handedly achieved more than my four sons,' a distant uncle complimented my father.

'You are a fortunate man, Subir,' praised another. 'I wish I had a son like yours.'

'I have decided,' an aunt broke in at this juncture. 'I am

putting Indranil in the NDA.'

Indranil was her son and a distant cousin of mine.

These were the same people who had once scorned my choice, saying that the army was for those who couldn't do anything else. I was happy that I had heralded a new profession in the family where only doctors and engineers commanded respect.

Although he didn't admit it, my father grudgingly allowed his chest to swell up by a few inches.

'After all he is my son,' he proudly announced one evening at a party where his friends were discussing the feats of their sons.

It was then that I realized how much I had learnt in the two and a half years I had spent at the Academy, much more than most people did in their entire lifetime.

I allowed the praise to get to my head. It felt good to hear the nice things after I had faced the stiff resistance to the career of my choice. But even praise can get tiresome after a while, I realized as the days passed.

I was beginning to get restless. I wanted to be back at the Academy.

My parents also sensed the change in me. 'You are no longer the same,' my mom accused me. 'You don't enjoy being at home.'

'That is not true,' I defended myself. 'It is just that I miss my friends at the Academy.'

I had never missed the Academy so much. It had been my home for two and a half long years, and now, just six more months remained before I moved out of it forever. We were now in our sixth term.

Happiness surged through my veins as the familiar portal of the Academy loomed up in the distance. It was like homecoming. Randy was sitting on an easy chair in the sun outside the squadron when I reached there. We greeted each other like long lost friends, and I sat down across him. A dreamy look suffused his face as he looked at the squadron.

'Life at any place other than here seems so uncomfortable. This is more our home than the real one,' he mused. He had spoken the very words that were lingering on my lips.

'It kind of makes me sad that we'll have to leave after six months,' I agreed.

The two of us sat in silence watching the Sudan Block in the distance.

'The devil arrives,' I said, spotting Bertie entering the squadron. After we had hugged each other, he dumped the luggage in his cabin, and we proceeded for lunch. The Academy looked like a ghost town. The first-termers were to arrive the next day.

By the time we ended our lunch, Maachh and Natty had also arrived. It was a joyous reunion for the gang. We greeted each other with unprecedented bonhomie.

Maachh was full of his escapades at the local club, and the thundering ovation he had managed at the boxing competition there. He flexed his puny biceps and boasted about the conquest, while Bertie shared his experiences about the beaches of Goa.

'The white females are so uninhibited,' he gushed. 'They loll around half naked on the sands, making the boys gape. During this break, I did a lot of gaping, too.'

'I will accompany you during the next break,' declared Maachh.

'That is if I take you with me,' retorted Bertie. The two were always at loggerheads, and that had not changed with time.

Some things never change – for instance, the deputy's obsession with bettering the quality of the cadets' lives. He wanted to bring in radical reforms. A smoker himself, he permitted all sixth-termers to smoke openly in the squadrons.

His announcement shocked everyone. There were those who opined that allowing the cadets to smoke openly would send the NDA up in smoke. Some felt that the sixth-termers who did not smoke would also start smoking. Most instructors thought it would be setting a bad precedent.

The permission to smoke, however, worked otherwise. Suddenly, the magic of smoking faded away. Many sixth-termers gave up smoking and the number of smokers went down drastically. It was one thing to steal a smoke on the sly, and another to smoke openly. The thrill of doing the forbidden was what made most cadets smoke.

Our nightly meetings inside the tank for a smoke had also lost the thrill. I gave up smoking, and so did Randy.

'Smoking has become boring. The deputy has ruined the charm,' I said one night inside the tank.

'I'll take to cigars', announced Randy. 'Smoking a cigar is classy. It has style.'

'Yeah, like Fidel Castro,' Bertie agreed.

'In that case, I will take to smoking a pipe,' I laughed. 'Like Sherlock Holmes.'

'Where will you get your tobacco supply from?' asked Bertie, 'Gole Market doesn't stock any.'

'While you guys decide on the subject, I have found some alternatives. Take your pick,' said Maachh fishing out snuff and some paan masala from his pocket. 'Multiple choice!'

He passed it around, but there were no takers.

'This is no officer material; it is degrading stuff, Maachh. I am not into this; count me out,' Randy stated disdainfully.

'Bidi?'

'No,' we shouted in unison. 'We'd better not lower our standards to that of Raju.' Raju was the room orderly who was addicted to bidis, but occasionally enjoyed a little bit of 'ganja' and hash, as well.

'How about tharra?' quipped Bertie. 'We could try it again. The aim is to get a kick, isn't it? In fact, I don't mind hash, ganja or tharra. What says Pessi?'

'I wouldn't mind taking a shot,' I agreed.

We all agreed that life inside the battle tank was dull without some kicking agent. The idea of ganja excited us.

'That is real grown-up stuff. A fag is for kids,' said Bertie.

'I know where to get all the stuff you want,' bragged Maachh. 'Anything you guys want to try out – ganja, hash, whatever, just let me know.'

Maachh was serious. When I said I was willing to try anything, I was just posturing.

Ganja and hash were prohibited, and getting caught with it could get us thrown out of the Academy. Smoking was a minor issue that invited a few punishments, but this was hard stuff not worth the risk. I waited for someone else to sound the warning alarm this time. I didn't like the Gandhi label.

Unfortunately, no one spoke against the idea.

'We can try them out,' Said Randy. 'Just once, and no more.'

Maachh took the onus of acquiring the stuff. 'I'll bring the stuff to the tank tomorrow, after dinner,' he told us.

No one asked him how and from where he would acquire it.

The next night, there was excitement as we gathered inside the battle tank after dinner, and waited for Maachh to arrive. The tank had been our companion through thick and thin. It would have a wonderful story to narrate if only it could speak.

This was the place where we had bared our souls, shared our dreams of the future, frustrations, and elation. The mammoth structure of metal had been privy to our heartbreaks and adventures, as well as achievements and joys. The other cadets had similar haunts where a few close friends would gather. We knew of groups sitting on the garage roofs, on treetops far from the squadrons. Some went off as far as the 'Hut of Remembrance' and the playfields – isolated spots along the peripheral road.

'What's keeping Maachh?' said Randy.

'The guy must have got cold feet,' retorted Bertie.

It was almost an hour since dinner, but he hadn't turned up. Finally, we decided to call it a day, and returned to the squadron. Just as we were entering the squadron, there was the sound of screeching brakes, and Captain Sabharwal sprang out of his jeep.

'Cadet Randhir Singh,' he barked. 'Come here.'

My heart grew cold with foreboding as Randy walked towards the officer. Sabby wanted the entire squadron out in the parade ground. No reason was given for the sudden infliction of such an order.

All sixth-term appointments, including Bertie and I, went round taking stock of the cadets after the entire squadron had assembled. There were some seven cadets missing, and this number included Maachh.

We waited patiently for the seven cadets to turn up. The cadets had to be in by 10.00 p.m., and it was around 9.50 p.m.

By 10.00 p.m., the missing cadets, including Maachh, had arrived. All the cadets were made to line up in two rows, all along the parade ground.

It was a dark night. With only a solitary street lamp lighting it up, visibility on the parade ground was poor.

As I crossed the sixth-termers, Maachh tugged at my sleeves. He pulled me closer and whispered nervously, 'Pessi, I am in trouble.' He was literally shaking with anxiety, ready to collapse.

'What is it? Tell me, fast,' I said, looking around fearfully. I need not have worried. Captain Sabharwal was right at the other end, walking around the first-term cadets.

'A drug peddler is sitting inside Sabby's jeep. He is the guy I met for collecting the hash. The guy is supposed to identify the purchaser.' Maachh said in a trembling voice.

I knew immediately that it was an identification parade. Maachh had to be saved. Somehow, I had to pull him out of the identification parade.

After Randy counted and reported to Sabby that all the

cadets were present, Sabby pulled out the drug peddler from the jeep, and made him stand in front of the squadron.

'You guys are in trouble,' announced Sabby angrily. 'This guy has handed over some ganja to one of the cadets. Who is it? Own up!' he commanded.

No one did.

'One last chance. After this minute, if that guy is caught, I'll ensure that he goes home.' Sabby sounded the warning bell. It reverberated dangerously inside Maachh's brain. He began trembling all over again.

Office holders were free to roam around. Taking advantage of my freedom, I stood next to Maachh and held his hand tight. He was shaking violently. The axe, hammer, and sword, all were hanging clearly on Maachh's head. It was Judgement Day for the poor fellow. The last trumpet had sounded, and all that remained was the verdict.

There was pin-drop silence. Then Sabby pushed the guy towards the first-termers, and the identification parade began. The chap looked totally confused. It was almost impossible to differentiate between the cadets. With their crop-cut hair, and uniforms, everybody looked alike. Besides, he had had just a brief glimpse of his customer.

From the first-termers to the second and then the third, the baffled peddler traipsed uncertainly. Just as Sabby stepped towards the sixth-termers, I pulled out Maachh from the group, and taking advantage of the darkness pushed him behind the garage, which was just about five metres away. He lay motionless there till the peddler had gone past the sixth- termers.

Unable to identify anyone, the drug peddler gave our squadron a clear chit, and pushed off to Hunter squadron where a similar drill was to follow. It was conducted all over the Academy, but the guy failed to identify the erring cadet.

It took a long time for Maachh to recover from the shock.

'Never again,' he vowed solemnly. 'I will never attempt another contact with the guy.'

We got to know the entire story the next day. Maachh had contacted the peddler through Raju, who regularly bought the stuff from him. Although Maachh had requested Raju for the hash, the orderly had clearly refused to get involved in the deal.

'I will just set up a meeting between the two of you, nothing more,' he had said sternly. 'If the deputy finds out that I have anything to do with this business, I will lose my job.'

So, Raju had set up a meeting between the two behind the dhobi ghat. Unknown to both Raju and Maachh, an officer and a couple of ustaads had been lying in wait for the peddler – they had prior information about the chap's activities. As soon as Maachh had reached the place, and the peddler had made his appearance, the security chaps stepped in. Maachh, who was a nimble chap, had sprinted away in the darkness, but the peddler had been caught. For once, Maachh was thankful for the cross-country practice sessions.

Naturally, there was no more talk of ganja, charas or hash, after that. We were content with an occasional puff of the fag or a sip from the bottle of Goan feni that Bertie occasionally produced from nowhere.

A little while later, it was time for another camp. 'Camp Torna', held in the sixth term, was something we all looked forward to. The two previous camps – Greenhorn and Rover – had been tough but enjoyable, and we were more than ready for the third one.

Torna, of course, was more of a challenge than anything we had gone through. It took the steam off the most adventurous cadets. *You are in the last term*, the instructors never failed to remind us sadistically.

The routine was gruelling. The daily long marches, which Randy referred to as Dandi marches, were rather tough on our feet and bodies.

'You should be enjoying the Dandi marches, our dear Gandhi,' they teased. The joke was on me.

The day before the campfire, we went on another long march. When we retired for the day, we were about fourteen kilometres away from a place called Maruni. When Natty heard of this village, he was extremely excited. His elder brother Harish, after his probation with Indian Overseas Bank at Bombay, was posted there. One of the chief regrets in Natty's life was that he had not been able to attend his brother's marriage, which had taken place just the previous month. Worse, he had not met his sister-in-law nor enjoyed the affection and jokes that the relationship offered. All he had seen were pictures of the wedding that his brother had sent.

'Imagine, coming so close to Harish's place and not being able to meet him,' lamented Natty.

'If I were you I would have hiked up to Maruni and met him,' said Randy.

'Are you crazy? We have already walked hundreds of kilometres, and Maruni is another fourteen kilometres away. The guy will collapse,' I vetoed the idea.

'Correction, Pessi! We have not walked hundreds of kilometres. We are not Alexander's soldiers,' reminded Randy. 'Besides, what is the use of all the training if he can't trudge up another fourteen?'

Both Maachh and Bertie seemed to agree with the idea.

'You could get us some sweets, while you are at it,' said Maachh, who had no remorse about sending the guy on Mission Impossible just so that he could indulge his sweet tooth.

Natty looked doubtful. 'Even if I walked all the way, it would take me a long time, and I wouldn't be able to return before morning.'

'Of course you could. Just keep running like the character in the movie *The Longest Day* or was it *The Longest Night*?' asked Maachh.

'Why don't you come with me?' said Natty, annoyed. 'That

way you will get to eat the sweets, and I will have company.' That wiped the smirk off Maachh's face.

'Look, tomorrow we have a virtually free day.' Randy was thoughtful. 'There are no marches on the agenda. Only the preparations for the campfire are on the schedule. I think you can make it.'

He was trying his best to motivate the guy. Although Natty was reluctant because the route involved going over a hillock, and wooded area with only a footpath marked on the map, the thought of meeting his brother and sister-in-law, tempted him to consider the idea.

Finally, it was decided that he would leave the camp at about 3.00 in the morning, so that he would be there by 6.00, and after breakfast with his brother, he could start again. We would hold the fort in his absence.

Natty had a harrowing experience. After the gruelling journey through the hillocks and wooded area, he managed to reach the village when the sun was peeping out of its hideout. His dress was in an awful state, torn by brambles at some places. His hair looked unkempt, and he had not shaved either. The shoes and trousers were stained with mud and muck. He looked like a miserable tramp. He washed himself at the public tube well, smartened himself up as best as he could, and went around asking about his brother.

At last he found the house and pressed the doorbell. A lady opened the door, and Natty recognized her immediately. She was his sister-in-law. Before he could utter a word, she vanished, leaving him at the door. Natty thought she had gone to call his brother. Nothing of the sort happened. His sister-in-law returned, alone, with a chapatti and a couple of coins.

Natty could not understand what hit him. He quietly put forth his hand, and accepted the alms that his sister-in-law offered, mistaking him to be a beggar. It was an anti-climax to his fourteen-kilometre-long rough hike through hard terrain.

Stunned, he turned back, and headed for the camp. He was still shaking his head in disbelief as he approached us.

TWENTY-ONE

The days flew, and the term seemed to pass too soon for our liking. One of the activities that became frequent in the sixth term was firing. We had to cycle down to the firing range with our rifles, and fire the whole day.

The firing range was totally barren and devoid of any kind of vegetation. The nearest tree, with sparse foliage, was about a 100 metres away. With the noon sun shining mercilessly overhead, the ustaads scrambled for cover under the nearest tree, while the officer read books in the shade of his tent, which had been pitched at a vantage spot overlooking the firing range.

For the cadets, there was no respite. Dust, heat, and the loud, deafening pounding was our lot.

One noon, we were firing on four feet x four feet targets placed at a distance of 100 metres. As we continued firing, an unusually heavy cloud of dust covered one side of the range.

Captain Sabharwal, who was reading his favourite author's novel *The Prodigal Daughter*, noticed from a distance that a cadet was firing grossly off the mark. As the rounds landed far and wide, the impact of their fall raised dust. Not willing to relinquish the book, which had reached an interesting turn, he rushed with the novel to the range where the cadets were firing. To Sabby's misfortune, the Fü hrer had decided on an inspection of the firing range, that noon.

The deputy headed straight for Sabharwal and ordered an immediate halt of the firing. Then he proceeded towards the target area with Sabby by his side. Tension mounted as the Fü hrer inspected the targets. Suddenly, the deputy stopped before a target. Shock clouded his features as he stared at the virgin target unmarked by a single bullet hole. While all the other targets had quite a number of hits, this one was shining clean. He snorted angrily and barked, 'Whose target is this?'

It was Maachh's target. The poor guy began trembling and tried to hide behind Captain Sabharwal.

The Fü hrer looked at Sabharwal squarely, and in a voice dripping with acid, said, 'Captain, you are an asset to the enemy, and with the guys you are training, especially the one trying to hide behind you,' pointing at Maachh, he continued, 'we'll definitely win the next war.'

Ferreira was never benign when confronted with such situations.

Sabharwal had no comments to offer. He gnashed his teeth, and threw deadly looks at Maachh, who was squirming with discomfort under the severe scrutiny.

'I'll be back in an hour, and if I don't see a marked improvement in that cadet's firing (hinting at Maachh), off you go, back to your regiment,' pronounced the deputy.

Before he sat in his car, he cautioned Sabharwal, 'And Captain, stop reading books on sons and daughters. Read military history, it will do you a lot more good.' He drove off, pumping a lot of dust into Sabharwal's stunned face.

Sabharwal stomped back to Maachh, who was waiting for

something terrible to happen. The captain was furious. He had been threatened and insulted by the deputy within the earshot of his cadets. He called Ustaad Bahadur Thapa, who was in charge of ammunition that day.

Thapa had won a silver medal at the Commonwealth Games in shooting. He was a professional trainer, and had a sharp eye for detail, a quality required by an instructor.

'Ustaad, charge sambhaal (Ustaad, take charge),' roared Sabharwal, pointing at Maachh.

Bahadur Thapa hollered at Maachh for a couple of minutes, then spent the next half an hour making him execute front-rolls, and an assortment of punishments. Sabharwal, who was watching all this, was getting restless as the deadline set up by the deputy was fast approaching. He kept gazing at his watch, while the ustaad continued punishing Maachh instead of getting down to business and making him fire.

Sabharwal was quite worried. There was just half an hour before the Fü hrer returned, and Maachh had not yet commenced firing. 'Theek hai, ustaad, ab aap isko practise karayen (That's enough, ustaad. Now get this chap to practise),' he commanded the ustaad, his patience finally giving way.

With hardly fifteen minutes to go before the Fü hrer returned, the ustaad pushed Maachh, who was panting and sweating by now, to the firing point.

Maachh assumed the firing position, and just as he was about to fire, the ustaad gave him a tight shove, 'Is this the way you take aim?' he yelled, 'Where is your back-sight?'

Maachh had forgotten to lift the back-sight of the rifle, without which one cannot take aim. It was a technical fault and the canny eyes of Bahadur Thapa had detected the flaw right from the beginning. No wonder he had sadistically subjected Maachh to all sorts of punishment for almost forty-five minutes, while Sabharwal sweated.

The deputy arrived exactly after an hour, confident that Maachh would still be shooting off the target, and he would get an opportunity to holler at Sabby. But Maachh, now with the back-sight of his SLR up, fired with cool confidence. All rounds hit the target, and the Fü hrer was amazed at the tight grouping Maachh had achieved.

Flummoxed at the sudden improvement in Maachh's firing, he went around the target twice. 'Amazing!' he finally declared, unable to find any faults. 'What did you do in just an hour to turn an ass into a horse?' he asked.

Sabharwal, who was in a state of shock himself, had no answer. It was all Thapa's doing, anyway.

'Excellent work, Captain,' proclaimed the deputy. 'I take back my words.'

He went on to reward Sabby by announcing , 'I confer on you the responsibility of training the NDA firing team.'

The Fü hrer was still shaking his head in disbelief as he walked back to his car.

Elated at the honour, Sabharwal did not know whether to thank or curse Maachh.

Trouble followed Maachh like Samson trailed Delilah.

Three days after the firing range incident, he fell off his horse while riding. Kabutar, normally a well-behaved horse, suddenly decided to buck while Maachh was trying to coax it into a faster trot. The Tragedy King had a bad fall and dislocated a bone in his left arm.

He was rushed to the hospital where, much to Maachh's consternation, Manisha took charge of him. 'What have I done to deserve Madame Cruella's prescription?' he wailed pathetically.

Our pal was admitted in the hospital for a couple of days to keep him from further mishaps.

'It is great to be admitted in the hospital,' he grinned when we visited him in the evening. 'No fear of the deputy or any punishment.

It is cool here, man. I am enjoying myself.'

'Hasn't Cruella been at her job?' we asked.

'On the contrary, she's been a ministering angel.'

'I think I will fall off a horse during my next riding class,' declared Bertie. 'Then you will have company.'

'NO! Don't you dare!' threatened Maachh. 'I don't want any disturbance here. Besides, I have fallen in love.'

'Not with Cruella DeVille again,' we exclaimed in unison. 'She will ensure that all your bones are broken and you remain bedridden for your entire life,' warned Randy.

'That battleship! No, yaar, it is not Manisha this time. I am not an idiot although I may look like one,' he assured us. 'You should meet Leena. She looks like Rekha, walks like Zeenat Aman, and talks like Sharmila Tagore.'

'Oh my! A living museum, you mean. What a confusing combo,' groaned Bertie. 'Who is this cocktail?'

'She is a nurse here.' We caught Maachh blushing.

'Does she give you a bath?' asked Randy.

'Only medicine.'

'What about an injection on your *gluteus maximus*?' I couldn't resist the wisecrack.

'Gluteee ... What's that?' our friend was baffled.

'Never mind, it is just the biological name for buttocks,' explained Randy with a straight face.

'No jokes, I am serious, guys,' Maachh admonished us. 'Can't you people ever take me seriously? Bertie fell in love, didn't he? You didn't make fun of him then. If I fall in love, it is fun time for you chaps.'

He looked genuinely hurt, so we cheered him up with the latest news about the squadron.

The week-long stay at the hospital did Maachh plenty of good. He looked relaxed and cheerful. We asked him about the nurse the moment he got back.

'Did you get the green signal?'

'No yaar, she went red when I asked if I could meet her some time. She has a boyfriend already.'

'How sad,' said Bertie.

'And I believed myself to be irresistible,' sighed our man. Maachh managed to stay cool about the entire affair. 'There will be other girls at other times. Life is too short to moon about,' he ended philosophically, and we all agreed whole-heartedly.

TWENTY-TWO

The DLTGH (days left to go home) were steadily decreasing, from triple digits to two digits, and then there were just ten days remaining before the term ended. All our tests were over, and preparations for the POP were set in motion. The mood was relaxed. Parents of all sixth-termers received invitations to the POP, and my parents made their train reservations to attend the function.

'The only thing I am scared about is the squadron social after which we will get our share of thrashing from the juniors,' remarked Bertie, letting out a spiral ring of smoke from his fag.

We had assembled inside the battle tank after a hearty dinner. At teatime, the discussions invariably swung to the topic of thrashing. All the sixth-termers were going through severe stress in anticipation of the event.

Ravi was sure to get a sound thrashing. All CSMs did, and he was no exception. He had resigned himself to his fate. Unlike us, who had given up punishing the juniors a long time back, he continued doling out punishments as if there was no tomorrow. He couldn't be blamed. As a CSM, it was his job to ensure discipline, but this spurred some of the youngsters to give him broad hints about his fate after the impending social.

The CSM and the CQMS were always the prime targets for the juniors. The CSM this time, was in for severe punishment because he was generally the harshest of disciplinarians, and the CQMS because he and his friends pigged on the juniors' share of evening snacks. He had put on a lot of weight during his sixth term, and the reason was quite obvious.

The CQMS was scared of the thrashing, so he turned a new leaf. He began restricting the sixth-termers from taking more than their share of the snacks during tea-time, but his attempts at atonement came a little too late.

My parents arrived two days before the POP. As usual, my father feigned indifference, but he couldn't help being impressed as he went around the Academy. My mother was gushing with enthusiasm. She was proud of my achievements.

The Echo squadron had been vacated for the parents of cadets who were to pass out. The freshly distempered and painted squadron was done up with flowers and new linen, and looked like a five-star hotel.

The schedule worked out for the parents was a hectic one. The day prior to the POP, they were shown a film on the Academy. Then there was a horse show, a polo match, and a PT display thrown in for good measure. Like everything else at the Academy, the events arranged for the parents also moved with clockwork precision. So packed was their schedule that it was only after dinner that I got to meet my parents.

On the morning of the POP, I went to meet my parents before heading for the parade. I sought their blessings, as this was an important day for me. I explained to my mother where I would be standing, so that she could locate me during the parade in the sea of cadets.

'I am a divisional cadet captain, so I will be carrying a cane.

You can spot me easily as I will be standing separate from the other cadets.'

'Outstanding, you mean,' she joked, and I could see pride well up in her eyes.

My parents had never seen me in uniform before. My mom hugged me, and my dad patted me on my shoulders. It was his way of conveying that he was proud of me. I discerned a mistiness in my mom's eyes as she looked at me.

Right through the parade, my eyes wandered all over the visitors' gallery, hunting for my parents. Finally, I located them. I saw my father pointing at me, while my mom waved excitedly. They were a witness to the world their son was entering. I felt intoxicated with happiness.

A sense of exultation flooded through my body as I stood there in the parade ground, ramrod straight, as if a hot iron had been rolled over my starched body. It was my last parade at the Academy.

The same parade, which had been a pain in our earlier terms, now brought tears to our eyes. The crowds clapped and cheered as we marched past them in a magnificent formation. As we climbed the stairs of the Quarterdeck for the Final Step, twelve fighter aircrafts, piloted by officers who had passed out from the Academy, thundered past, flying low over our heads. A befitting send off.

After the parade was over, we walked over to our parents. A grand tea had been arranged for the parents of sixth-termers, who had come to witness the parade. Bertie's, Maachh's, Randy's... everyone's parents were there to see their sons climb an important step towards becoming officers. Our parents met each other and there was a jubilant air in the Academy.

I took my parents to the G squadron to show them the cabin I had occupied. The soulful tune of a song floated over the squadron creating a melodramatic moment.

'Oh jaane waale, ho sake to lautke aana... (Oh departing one, if possible, come back again).'

The song never failed to draw tears in the eyes of the sixth-termers who were leaving the Academy.

Maachh, and Vittal sat crying on the staircase of the squadron. Dhillon, the deadly sikh, was also in tears. No one could imagine him crying. Ravi was sobbing loudly. This was one day when no one was ashamed of crying. We had suffered severe physical punishments, pain and humiliation, but had not allowed a drop of tears to fall through the past three years. Now, it was the day we had to leave the Academy, and no one cared to camouflage the tears.

The tight bond of three years had come to an end. I blinked back the tears manfully as I escorted my parents into the anteroom. There would be enough time to cry when they were not watching, I promised myself.

My turn came that night after everyone had gone to sleep. I sat alone on the staircase, and gave vent to the emotions that had been threatening to overflow through the day. I could suppress my tears no more.

As a small boy, I had wondered what I would do in life. While others of my age group had wanted to become teachers, bus conductors, traffic policemen, or pilots, I had known that these vocations were not for me. It came to me out of the blue when I was just seven. Some of my classmates from Loyala High School were the children of officers posted at NDA. They lived inside the campus, and I attended their birthday parties at the National Defence Academy. Even then it did not strike me that I wanted to join the Academy. And then I attended a POP. Once was not enough. I attended it again and again, year after year, convinced that one day I would be marching to the same tune. My mind was made up. I would join the Academy.

The dream had been accomplished. I joined the Academy as a boy, and here I was, departing as a man.

EPILOGUE

After our Passing Out Parade, all those who were to be commissioned into the army went on to do another year's training at the Indian Military Academy, Dehradun. For the air force cadets, the training was at Air Force Academy at Begumpet, and the naval cadets went to INS Shivaji, Lonavla.

By the time we got our commission in the army, things at the NDA had gone through a sea change. The minimum age went up by a year, and so did the minimum qualification. The boys who joined were not as green as we had been at the time of admission. As for training, the spotlight shifted to academics instead of the corporeal aspect. With technological advancements, it was essential to play up the brain, not just the brawn.

We joined the Academy after passing Class 10, at the age of fifteen or sixteen. Today, the minimum qualification is Class 12, and the age has risen to seventeen and eighteen. When we were at the Academy, there were just twelve squadrons, and now there are fifteen. The tough ragging is a thing of the past. Yet, there is so much that has not altered, and can never change.

I got commissioned into the Regiment of Artillery, and so did Maachh. Randy went to the Brigade of Guards, and Natty into Infantry, while Bertie drew the Corps of Electrical and Mechanical Engineers.

Years later, I bumped into Maachh by accident, at a cantonment in Siliguri. Randy died young, in a tragic accident. Of Bertie, I have no news. Natty is somewhere in the country existing peacefully, I guess. I also met Manisha at the Military Hospital in the capital. Married to a neuro-surgeon in the army, she is now a cardiologist, mending hearts instead of wounding them. Much water has flowed under the bridge since our last encounter.

Today, when I see the young officers emerging from the Academy, I realize with a pang, that these guys are far smarter for their age than we ever were. Perhaps, it is in keeping with the present generation of human beings. The traditions, nevertheless, continue.

Although the names have been changed, the incidents, barring a couple of them, are true. I have no doubts that any of the course mates reading this book will recognize the characters immediately.